ONE MAN, TWO GUVNORS

Richard Bean

ONE MAN, TWO GUVNORS

Based on *The Servant of Two Masters*
by Carlo Goldoni

OBERON BOOKS
LONDON

WWW.OBERONBOOKS.COM

First published in 2011 by Oberon Books Ltd

US version first published in 2012 by Oberon Books Ltd
521 Caledonian Road, London N7 9RH
Tel: +44 (0) 20 7607 3637 / Fax: +44 (0) 20 7607 3629
e-mail: info@oberonbooks.com
www.oberonbooks.com

A catalogue record for this book is available from the British
Library.

PB ISBN: 9781849433846
E ISBN: 9781849432825

Cover image:
Photograph by Hugo Glendinning
Design by Spotco

Printed, bound and converted
by CPI Group (UK) Ltd, Croydon, CR0 4YY.

Visit www.oberonbooks.com to read more about all our books
and to buy them. You will also find features, author interviews and
news of any author events, and you can sign up for e-newsletters
so that you're always first to hear about our new releases.

This version of Goldoni's *The Servant of Two Masters* was developed from a comprehensive and detailed literal translation from the Italian by Francesca Manfrin.

I'd like to thank Didi Hopkins for her inspirational explanations of *Commedia*, and all who contributed to the script in the rehearsal room – you know who you are.

The lyrics for *Tomorrow Looks Good From Here* were co-written with Grant Olding.

Richard Bean

Characters

CHARLIE 'CHARLIE THE DUCK' CLENCH
50s, Brighton based but originally London
(Pantalone)

PAULINE CLENCH
his daughter, Brighton (Clarice)

HARRY DANGLE
60s, crooked attorney, Rottingdean / tries to be
posh Brighton (Lombardi)
Partner in Dangle, Berry and Bush attorneys.

ALAN
the son of Dangle (Silvio)

DOLLY
30s, an employee of Clench, Brighton
(Smeraldina)

LLOYD BOATENG
50s, a friend to Clench, Ex London/Jamaican
(Brighella)

FRANCIS
Essex Boy
(Truffaldino)

RACHEL CRABBE
mid-20s, London (Beatrice Rasponi; 1st Master)

STANLEY STUBBERS
mid-20s, Home counties, privately educated
(Florindo Aretusi; 2nd Master)

Waiters/Porters as required

Notes on text
I'm not using continental scene changes, ie: the scene doesn't
change on the entrance of new character, rather scene changes
are restricted to time and location changes.

One Man, Two Guvnors was first performed at Lyttelton Theatre, National Theatre on the 17th May 2011 with the following cast:

GARETH, David Benson
STANLEY STUBBERS, Oliver Chris
ENSEMBLE, Polly Conway
FRANCIS HENSHALL, James Corden
ENSEMBLE, Jolyon Dixon
ALFIE, Tom Edden
HARRY DANGLE, Martyn Ellis
ENSEMBLE, Derek Elroy
LLOYD BOATENG, Trevor Laird
PAULINE CLENCH, Claire Lams
ENSEMBLE, Paul Lancaster
ENSEMBLE, Fergus March
ENSEMBLE, Gareth Mason
CHARLIE CLENCH, Fred Ridgeway
ALAN, Daniel Rigby
RACHEL CRABBE, Jemima Rooper
ENSEMBLE, Clare Thomson
DOLLY, Suzie Toase

Director, Nicholas Hytner
Associate Director, Cal McCrystal
Designer, Mark Thompson
Lighting Designer, Mark Henderson
Music, Grant Olding
Sound Designer, Paul Arditti
Fight Director, Kate Waters

One Man, Two Guvnors was first performed at Music Box Theatre, New York on the 6th April, 2012 with the following cast:

STANLEY STUBBERS, Oliver Chris
FRANCIS HENSHALL, James Corden
ALFIE, Tom Edden
HARRY DANGLE, Martyn Ellis
ENSEMBLE, Brian Gonzales
ENSEMBLE, Eli James
LLOYD BOATENG, Trevor Laird
PAULINE CLENCH, Claire Lams
GARETH, Ben Livingston
ENSEMBLE, Sarah Manton
ENSEMBLE, Stephen Pilkington
CHARLIE CLENCH, Fred Ridgeway
ALAN, Daniel Rigby
RACHEL CRABBE, Jemima Rooper
ENSEMBLE, David Ryan Smith
ENSEMBLE, Natalie Smith
DOLLY, Suzie Toase

Director, Nicholas Hytner
Physical Comedy Director, Cal McCrystal
Composer, Grant Olding
Designer, Mark Thompson
Lighting Designer, Mark Henderson
Sound Designer, Paul Arditti
Associate Director, Adam Penford
Original UK Casting, Alastair Coomer CDG
US Casting, Tara Rubin Casting CSA

New York Producers
Bob Boyett, National Theatre of Great Britain
under the direction of Nicholas Hytner and Nick Starr,
National Angels, Chris Harper, Tim Levy,
Scott Rudin, Roger Berlind, Harriet Leve, Stephanie P. McClelland,
Broadway Across America, Daryl Roth, Jam Theatricals,
Sonia Friedman, Harris Karma, Deborah Taylor, Richard Willis

Act One

SCENE ONE

As the audience take their seats the skiffle band plays. Lights down. 1963, April, mid morning. A room in CHARLIE's house in Brighton. A framed photo of Queen Elizabeth II at coronation upstage. CHARLIE, HARRY DANGLE, ALAN DANGLE, PAULINE, LLOYD, DOLLY and other friends and family. Hardly anything remains from a buffet of typically English party food. Maybe one lone cheese and pineapple on a stick, and some peanuts. A party can of beer etc. All very lively and jolly, with the skiffle band playing, laughter, drinks, dancing. The song finishes. PAULINE and ALAN kiss. They toast "Pauline & Alan" CHARLIE taps a glass for quiet.

DANGLE: Happy engagement! Pauline and Alan!

ALL: Pauline and Alan!

DOLLY: Come on Charlie! Give us a speech!

LLOYD: Speech!

CHARLIE: I've only ever spoken three times, formally,
in public, in my life, and each time I've been banged
up by the judge straight afterwards! For twenty years,
me and Pauline's mother, Jean, were happy, and then,
unfortunately, just by chance, we met each other. Alan,
you've decided to get married, and as a man who has been
married, I'd just like to say, I do hope you realize you're
making a terrible mistake.

ALL: *(Beat of concerned silence, then laughter.)*

CHARLIE: I done me best bringing up Pauline, on me own,
after her muvver… *(Chokes.)* …sorry…

LLOYD: – doin' well Charlie.

CHARLIE: – I've had to be her dad and her mum after her
muvver… *(Chokes.)*

PAULINE: – It's alright dad.

CHARLIE: – ...after her muvver left me and went to live in Spain. It's a disappointment that Jean can't be here in Brighton at her daughter's engagement party, and a shame she can't even afford a stamp for a card neither. But I'm not gonna go on about it. I'd like to thank Alan's father, my attorney.

DANGLE: *(Coming forward.) Ecce homo*!

CHARLIE: No Latin! Please! I have enough difficulty understanding you when you're speaking English. But, seriously, wivout Harry, I wouldn't be here today, I'd be behind bars, where, let's face it, by rights, I oughta be. Over to you Alan.

CHARLIE steps back. Applause for CHARLIE. ALAN kneels, with a flourish, before PAULINE.

ALAN: Pauline, I give you my hand. *(ALAN holds out an upturned, closed, cupped hand towards PAULINE.)*

DOLLY: *(Aside.)* He wants to be an actor.

ALAN: Captive within my hand, is a bird. This bird is my heart.

PAULINE: *(To DOLLY.)* Is it a real bird?

DOLLY: No. It's a metaphor.

PAULINE: *(Excited.)* Oh! Lovely!

ALAN: I offer you the whole of my life, as your husband.

DOLLY: *(Aside.)* Ooh! I could do with a bit of this myself.

PAULINE opens his hand and takes out the imaginary bird, and presses it to her heart.

PAULINE: I accept your bird heart thing, and I promise to look after it properly *(PAULINE kneels, and offers her hand to ALAN.)* I got a bird in my hand an'all.

PAULINE: – This bird is *my* heart, the only one I've ever had.

ALAN mimes taking the bird and presses it through his ribcage into his heart. They kiss passionately. Silence. A bit embarrassing. It is broken by the pop of a champagne cork.

DANGLE: May I propose a toast. To love! In Latin –

CHARLIE: – Oh no!

DANGLE: *Ars amandi!*

PAULINE: Not Mandy! Pauline.

ALAN: *(To PAULINE.)* "*Ars amandi*" is the art of love.

PAULINE: I don't understand.

ALAN: *(Aside.)* This is why I love her. She is pure, innocent, unsoiled by education, like a new bucket.

LLOYD: To love!

ALL: To love!

They toast. The doorbell rings.

CHARLIE: Dolly, get the door.

DOLLY: Bookkeeper? Or butler? Make your mind up.

CHARLIE: And if it's carol singers tell them to piss off. It's only April.

DOLLY exits.

LLOYD: You're Charlie's attorney?

They shake hands.

DANGLE: Harry Dangle. Dangle, Berry and Bush. My card.

LLOYD: *(Reading.)* No win, same fee?

DANGLE: That's us.

LLOYD: Charlie tells me you're good.

DANGLE: Put it this way, I got the Mau Mau off. Are you family Lloyd?

LLOYD: No, no! An old friend. Me and Charlie go way back.

(Aside.) Brixton prison.

PAULINE: Dad! Me and Alan, we're gonna go up to my room, to play some records.

CHARLIE: Do I look like I just came down in the last shower? No! Mingle!

LLOYD takes CHARLIE to one side. Gets out invitation.

LLOYD: Man! What's going on! Last week I gets this invitation to a *engagement* party –

CHARLIE: – put that away.

LLOYD: – of Pauline Clench and Roscoe Crabbe, which was a shock because I always thought Roscoe was, you know, homosexual.

CHARLIE: Of course he was. That was the whole point, it was gonna be a marriage of convenience.

LLOYD: But today and it's a different groom man!

CHARLIE: Because Roscoe's dead. Pauline and this Alan wanted to get engaged, so I thought –

LLOYD: – I've paid for the sausage rolls so why waste them?!

CHARLIE: Exactly!

Enter DOLLY, looking serious.

DOLLY: Some geezer from London. Says he's Roscoe's minder.

CHARLIE: Roscoe Crabbe's minder?

LLOYD: Can't be much of a minder, Roscoe's dead.

CHARLIE: Is he a face? Does he look handy?

DOLLY: To be honest, he looks a bit overweight.

CHARLIE: Check him out Lloydie, see if he's got a shooter.

LLOYD: Charlie, I don't work for you no more.

DOLLY: Leave it to me, boys. *(DOLLY exits.)*

DANGLE: More guests?

CHARLIE: Roscoe Crabbe's minder.

DANGLE: But I was led to understand there was a knife fight and Roscoe Crabbe was mortally wounded?

CHARLIE: No! He was killed.

LLOYD: Good riddens!

CHARLIE: The cops are looking for his twin sister, Rachel, and her boyfriend.

DANGLE: Because?

LLOYD: Revenge! The boyfriend testified against Roscoe in court. Put him away for four years. Man! It's obvious! Who is Roscoe gonna get into a fight with on his first day of freedom?

CHARLIE: *(To DANGLE, unnecessarily.)* Rachel's boyfriend.

Enter DOLLY.

DOLLY: He's clean. Shall I let him in?

CHARLIE: *(Nods.)* Yeah. *(Exit DOLLY.)* What can I do?

LLOYD: She's a smashing girl is Rachel! Notin' like that vicious little toerag of a brother!

CHARLIE: I think Roscoe was a bit whatsaname – you know, what's that word for someone who likes inflicting pain?

LLOYD: Police officer.

CHARLIE: No!

DANGLE: Sadist.

CHARLIE: That's Roscoe.

LLOYD: Unusual for twins to have such different personalities.

CHARLIE: *(To DANGLE.)* They was identical twins, you see, Roscoe and Rachel.

LLOYD: Roscoe was a boy, and Rachel is a girl!

CHARLIE: So?

DANGLE: Identical means identical.

CHARLIE: What I want to know is, if Roscoe's dead, what's his minder doing on my doorstep.

Enter DOLLY. Followed by FRANCIS. FRANCIS is suited and booted, but the suit is too tight, too short. The room freezes. FRANCIS is acting tough. FRANCIS checks the room as if looking for hidden dangers. He's playing the role of hard man minder. Everyone else is still, frozen in fear, waiting for a cue from CHARLIE. FRANCIS stops under the picture of the Queen. Points to it.

FRANCIS: Who's that?

PAULINE: That's the Queen.

FRANCIS: What a beautiful woman. Someone should write a song about her.

PAULINE: God Save the Queen?

FRANCIS: That's a good title.

FRANCIS picks a peanut from a bowl on the side and throws on in the air, catches it in his mouth.

PAULINE: This is my engagement party.

FRANCIS: *Your* engagement party. Phew!

(To DOLLY.) Phew 'cause I'm glad it ain't yours – "beautiful eyes".

DOLLY: Thank you.

FRANCIS: Don't ever wear glasses. Even if you need to, you know, for reading.

DOLLY: *(Aside.)* I know exactly what he's after, and if carries on like this he's gonna get it. *(FRANCIS throws a second peanut and catches that too. To FRANCIS.)* What about glasses for driving?

FRANCIS: Are you one of them women's libbers?

DOLLY: Would that be a problem?

FRANCIS: I like a woman who can drive. That way I can go out, get drunk, and get home without killing anyone. Are you married to er –

DOLLY: – I'm single, I'm the bookkeeper here.

FRANCIS: So you're a single, working, driving, bookkeeping woman. That's my type. Do want to go to Spain for a couple of weeks? Majorca. Think about it. *(FRANCIS throws a third peanut in the air which forces him to run backwards to catch it. He hits the sofa, goes over with it, and pops up the other side.)*

Got it.

He shows the peanut on his tongue.

DOLLY: *(Aside.)* I like this geezer. But he can't tell the difference between his arse and a Public Holiday.

FRANCIS: *(He approaches LLOYD.)* Alright man?! Do you like blues music? Muddy Waters. Robert Johnson. Leadbelly?

LLOYD: No.

FRANCIS: Oh. That's a shame. I do. What kind of music do you like?

LLOYD: Calypso.

FRANCIS: Oh dear! Dear oh dear. I can't stand Calypso.

FRANCIS offers his hand to be shaked. LLOYD shakes.

But! No hard feelings man. I want you to know, I'm on your side, in the struggle. Despite your disappointing taste in music.

DANGLE: *(To CHARLIE.)* This man is a clown.

FRANCIS turns on DANGLE grabbing his balls à la Vinnie Jones.

FRANCIS: Everybody at the circus loves the clowns. So, when you say "this man is a clown", what you're really saying is "I love you". Are you Charlie the Duck?

DANGLE: No.

FRANCIS: No?

DANGLE: No.

FRANCIS lets all the role playing drop, and becomes low status apologetic.

FRANCIS: Oh shit, have I got the wrong house? The invitation –

Gets his invitation out.

CHARLIE: – I'm Charlie the Duck.

FRANCIS: Right. Ok. You don't look like a duck.

CHARLIE: I know who you are. You're Roscoe Crabbe's minder.

FRANCIS: I am. And I have an invitation to his engagement party. This party.

CHARLIE: Roscoe's dead.

FRANCIS: If Roscoe's dead, who's that sitting outside in the motor, listening to the Shipping Forecast on the radio.

PAULINE rushes to the window.

PAULINE: Oh my God! No!

CHARLIE: He's risen from the dead has he?

FRANCIS: Yeah. It only took him two days. That's one day quicker than the previous world record. So?! Can he come in? To his own engagement party?

CHARLIE: I guess.

FRANCIS: I'll go and get him.

FRANCIS exits, with a wink to DOLLY. Voices are now raised...

PAULINE: Dad! No! Don't let him in! I love Alan, I don't love Roscoe, I never did.

CHARLIE: You was perfectly happy with Roscoe six month back.

DANGLE: He's missed the boat.

CHARLIE: Roscoe Crabbe can be as late as he likes. And we have an arrangement.

ALAN: An arranged marriage worthy of a Moliére farce, contemptible even in the seventeenth century.

PAULINE: Yeah, dad, this is the nineteenth century now!

CHARLIE: Yeah, well, what do you offer my daughter Alan? *I wanna be an actor.* You can't get more flakey!

ALAN: All I offer is love! My love for your daughter eclipses poetry. My love is ethereal, pure – like…like the kind of water you're supposed to put in a car battery.

Enter RACHEL, followed by FRANCIS. RACHEL is dressed as a fashionable young man, looking not unlike a short Ringo Starr.

RACHEL: Long time no see, Charlie.

They shake hands.

CHARLIE: Yeah. You look well Roscoe. All things considered. This is Lloyd, good friend of mine, Dolly, my bookkeeper, my attorney, Harry Dangle, he's good.

RACHEL: Are you the guy who got the Mau Mau off?

DANGLE: It wasn't easy.

CHARLIE: – and, 'course, you remember Pauline.

RACHEL: You look fantastic Pauline. *(ALAN walks in front of her, placing himself between her and RACHEL.)*

Who are you?

ALAN: Whole nations will be slain before you take my love from me.

RACHEL: *(To CHARLIE.)* Why's he talking like an actor?

DOLLY: He wants to be an actor.

RACHEL: Oh alright. Who are you then?

ALAN: I am your nemesis.

RACHEL: Francis! What's a nemesis?

FRANCIS: Dunno. Definitely foreign. I think it might be a Toyota.

RACHEL: *(Rachel goes over to CHARLIE, takes him downstage.)* What's going on Charlie?

CHARLIE: We thought you was dead.

RACHEL: If you thought I was dead, why would you go ahead with my engagement party?

CHARLIE: You know, I'd already paid for the sausage rolls and –

RACHEL: – IF YOU THOUGHT I WAS DEAD!?

CHARLIE: – The word was, you were murdered. Pauline's met someone else.

RACHEL: *(Indicating ALAN.)* Horror bollocks over there?

CHARLIE: Yeah.

RACHEL approaches ALAN.

RACHEL: So, let's have another go. What's your name?

ALAN: Alan.

RACHEL: I have a prior arrangement with Charlie and Pauline, Alan. It's not love, no, it can't be love. This is good news for you, Alan, because the deal guarantees Pauline complete freedom in affairs of the heart, as long as she is discrete.

ALAN: My love for Pauline is not discrete; it shouts from the rooftops "look at me, look at me, I am love!"

DANGLE: It shall be my son who marries Pauline. Come on Alan! We're going.

PAULINE: Don't leave me here Alan!

DANGLE: *(To CHARLIE.)* Mr Charles Clench, you will be hearing from me.

CHARLIE: I can explain.

ALAN: I shall return. Like a storm. And everybody will get wet.

ALAN exits. Door closed.

CHARLIE: Pauline. Over here. *(PAULINE is now crying. She goes downstage with CHARLIE.)*

Behave!

PAULINE: It's 1963 dad! You can't force me to marry a dead homosexual!

CHARLIE: He's not dead is he.

PAULINE: He is a homosexual though!

CHARLIE: We've only got his word for that. *(PAULINE runs off into another room. CHARLIE follows.)* Come back here!

(To ROSCOE.) Gimme a minute Roscoe.

CHARLIE, following PAULINE. He closes the door. During the next scene FRANCIS mimes taking out his pulsing heart and offering it to DOLLY.

RACHEL: Lloyd Boateng. My sister worked the bar for you at the The Palm Tree.

LLOYD: Rachel, yeah. What's she doing?

RACHEL: She's runs this nightclub now. It's her boyfriend's. The Stiletto, Mile End.

LLOYD: I've heard it's rough. Criminals, gangsters, Princess Margaret.

RACHEL: Rachel met him at York Hall. He was on the card. He won by a second round knockout. He'd boxed at his boarding school apparently.

LLOYD: I like your sister. She's a great girl.

RACHEL: And, she likes you. A lot. She said you could be trusted.

FRANCIS now fiddles with the nipples of an African woman sculpture. FRANCIS thinks this is a private thing between he and DOLLY but LLOYD and RACHEL watch. CHARLIE re-enters.

CHARLIE: The kid's upset. She thought you was dead. D'yer wanna sandwich?

FRANCIS: Yes! Yes please. We had to skip breakfast you see.

RACHEL: We're going to eat later. What's your understanding of the deal Charlie?

CHARLIE: I settle the debt I owed your father, paid to you on the day of your engagement –

RACHEL: – Six thousand two hundred today.

CHARLIE: Pauline, as your public wife, gets two grand a year, for attending functions on your arm.

RACHEL: Have you got the money Charlie?

CHARLIE: I'll write you a cheque out now. Six thousand two hundred.

RACHEL: Cashier's cheque. And I'll take the two hundred in cash.

CHARLIE: Dolly, phone the bank, get 'em to knock up a cashier's cheque for six grand.

DOLLY: *(Incredulous.)* For six thousand?

CHARLIE: That's what I said, yeah. *(DOLLY leaves. On the way she is aware of FRANCIS goosing her.)* Are you boys staying in Brighton?

RACHEL: Can you recommend somewhere?

LLOYD: I certainly can. The Cricketers Arms.

FRANCIS: Do they do sandwiches?

CHARLIE: Wash your mouth out! It's a pub, that does food. Lloyd is the landlord. He's had a three year training as a chef.

LLOYD: *(Aside.)* Brixton prison.

FRANCIS: That has got to be the most beautiful sentence in the English language. *A pub that does food.*

RACHEL: Francis, go ahead in the motor.

FRANCIS makes to leave.

What are you doing mate? You don't know where the pub is.

FRANCIS: Guv! For a pub that does food, there'll be a star in the sky.

FRANCIS leaves. DOLLY re-enters.

DOLLY: I've got the Bank on the phone.

CHARLIE: *(To RACHEL.)* I don't know why they want to talk to me. What's the problem. *(CHARLIE exits.)*

LLOYD: Rachel?

RACHEL: You're looking pretty good Lloydie!

LLOYD: Girl!? What all dis wid de rude boy disguise!

RACHEL: The Old Bill are looking for me. Can I trust you?

LLOYD: You're like a daughter to me!

RACHEL: My brother, Roscoe is dead. My boyfriend killed my twin brother, yeah. I should hate Stanley for that. But I love him. Have you ever been in love Lloyd?

LLOYD: True love? Yes, once.

(Aside.) Brixton prison.

Enter CHARLIE, in coat, and hat.

CHARLIE: I'm gonna go raise that two hundred folding.

CHARLIE's gone.

RACHEL: Me and Stanley are going to have to go to Australia.

LLOYD: Australia! No Man! Oh my God, no. that's really terrible. Australia. You poor thing girl! Why Australia? Do you like opera?

RACHEL: Not especially. But we've no choice. We sail from
Southampton on Monday. The morning tide. The police
will be watching the ports so –

LLOYD: – Brighton's near enough but safer?

RACHEL: And Charlie the Duck lives here, and we need
money.

LLOYD: I guess. Where is your Stanley now?

RACHEL: Brighton, somewhere. I've left a letter for him at
the post office with instructions for a rendezvous. I pray to
God he's alright.

End of Scene.

SCENE TWO

*Outside The Cricketers Arms Pub tables, and a dustbin. Enter FRANCIS
from the pub entrance.*

*On the pub table are some unfinished drinks. Some dregs of Guinness,
white wine, red wine in a bottle, orange juice etc.*

FRANCIS: My Father, Tommy Henshall, God rest his soul, he
woulda been proud of me, what I done with my life, until
today. I used to play washboard in a skiffle band, but they
went to see The Beatles last Tuesday night, and sacked
me Wednesday morning. Ironic, because I started The
Beatles. I saw them in Hamburg. Rubbish. I said to that
John Lennon, I said "John, you're going nowhere mate,
it's embarrassing, have you ever considered writing your
own songs". So I'm skint, I'm busking, guitar, mouth organ
on a rack, bass drum tied to me foot, and the definition
of mental illness, cymbals between my knees. So there I
am, middle of Victoria Station, I've only been playing ten
minutes, this lairy bloke comes over, he says – "do you
do requests?" I say "yes" he says "I'd like you to play a
song for my mother". I said "no problem, where is she?"
He said "Tazmania." So I nutted him. This little bloke
Roscoe Crabbe seen all this and offers me a week's work in
Brighton, says he needs a bit of muscle. I tell him this is all

fat. But I need a wage, I haven't eaten since last night. But I don't get paid until the end of the week, and I can't stop thinking about FISH AND CHIPS. I'm staying in a pub, and I don't even have enough shrapnel for a PINT.

He empties all the dregs into one pint pot picks a tab end out and downs it in one. He looks at the dustbin. Puts a hand on the lid.

There might be a discarded bag of chips in here. No! I can't go through the bins! Must stop thinking about FISH AND CHIPS. Come on Francis! Think about something boring, like… Canada.

He gives up. Lifts the lid and starts searching in the bin. Enter STANLEY STUBBERS. He is followed by a TAXI DRIVER carrying one big trunk.

TAXI DRIVER: That's as far as I'm going with this mate. *(The TAXI DRIVER puts the trunk down unceremoniously.)* The fare is five and six.

STANLEY: Oh Foot and Mouth! Don't be a bad egg about it!

STANLEY gives him the money.

TAXI DRIVER: I drive a taxi mate, I ain't Heracles.

STANLEY: It's a trunk. No one's asking you to hold up the sky for all eternity!

TAXI DRIVER: *Atlas* held up the sky. Heracles took over for five minutes so Atlas could go and get the golden apples from the Hesperides' garden.

The TAXI DRIVER leaves. STANLEY spots FRANCIS.

STANLEY: What's this pub like?

FRANCIS: Groundbreaking. It does food.

STANLEY: A pub? That does food?! Buzz-wam, whoever thought of that? Wrap his balls in bacon and send him to the nurse! What are the rooms like?

FRANCIS: World class.

STANLEY: Not that I care. I'm boarding school trained. I'm happy if I've got a bed, a chair, and no one pissing on my face. Could you do me a favour and keep an eye on the trunk for me, whilst I see if they have any vacancies?

FRANCIS: How much?

STANLEY: Half a crown?

FRANCIS: *(Aside.)* HADDOCK AND CHIPS AND MUSHY PEAS!

Yeah, alright.

STANLEY goes in to the pub. FRANCIS considers the trunk, and the task in hand. Enter an OLD WOMAN on sticks, struggling along. She looks, en passant, at the trunk.

FRANCIS: Don't even think about it.

The OLD WOMAN heads off towards stage right, and then stops, turns and looks. FRANCIS lets out a war cry, and charges him. The OLD WOMAN picks her sticks up and runs off. FRANCIS's charge takes him off stage right. A VICAR walks on and inspects the abandoned trunk. A blood-curdling scream from FRANCIS and he is projected on to the stage from stage right doing athletic full salto tumbling chasing the VICAR off into the wings stage left. FRANCIS walks back on, from stage left, straightening his tie. Enter STANLEY, acting secretively.

STANLEY: *(Loud whisper.)* I need, what they call in the army, a batman. What's a decent drink for a geezer like you, for a day's graft?

FRANCIS: My current guvnor, that is my *previous* guvnor, used to pay me twenty pounds a week, at the end of the week, which is no use to me.

STANLEY: Why not?

FRANCIS: I have to EAT EVERY DAY!

STANLEY: I shall pay you five pounds per day

FRANCIS: *(To STANLEY.)* Alright guv, you're on.

STANLEY: Do you know where the main Post Office is in Brighton?

FRANCIS: *(Aside.)* I have absolutely no idea.

Oh yeah, it's next door to my gran's.

STANLEY: There should be some post for me. You'll need this letter of authorisation.

STANLEY gives FRANCIS a letter.

FRANCIS: *(Reading.)* To whom it may concern, the bearer is an authorised agent of Stanley Stubbers.

STANLEY: Shhh!

FRANCIS: Who's Stanley Stubbers?

STANLEY: *(Whisper.)* Me! But don't call me Stanley Stubbers. I'm going to have to make up a new name for the pub.

FRANCIS: *(Whisper.)* What's wrong with "The Cricketers Arms?"

STANLEY: *(Whisper.)* You're not exactly a Swiss watch are you? A false name for me, because I'm lying low. What do I call you? I don't do first names. First names are for girls and Norwegians.

FRANCIS: *(Whisper.)* Henshall.

STANLEY: Like it! *(Whisper.)* Get my trunk indoors, Henshall, collect my letters Henshall. I'll be in my room.

(Exit STANLEY into the pub. Trunk Lazzi. FRANCIS attempts to move the trunk, it is too heavy. He requests help from the audience. Two volunteers are brought up onto the stage and are taught correct trunk lifting technique. Under instruction from FRANCIS they carry the trunk off into the pub.)

FRANCIS: Post office.

RACHEL: Oi! Francis! Where are you going mate?

FRANCIS: I'm walking round and round in circles to ward off the hunger pangs.

LLOYD: I will cook you the lunch of a lifetime.

FRANCIS: Lunch!? I haven't had breakfast yet.

RACHEL: Have you got my trunk out of the motor yet?

FRANCIS: I've just done the trunk.

(Aside.) Ah! – Concentrate Francis!

(To RACHEL.) Don't worry Roscoe, I'll get your trunk from the motor, now.

LLOYD: I'll get one of the bar staff to give you a hand. *(Exit LLOYD into the pub. He sees the two volunteers standing offstage.)* What! You two again! I've told you before, it's not that kind of pub! Come on out. *(The volunteers return to their seats.)*

RACHEL: I need you to go to the Post Office, and –

FRANCIS: – alright guv, stop going on about it. You only have to tell me once.

RACHEL: I haven't asked you to go to the Post Office at all, yet.

FRANCIS: *(Aside.)* Oh shit!

RACHEL: Lloyd tells me it is just around the corner.

FRANCIS: *(Aside.)* That's handy.

RACHEL: Collect any letters for me or my sister, Rachel Crabbe. This is a letter of authorisation.

FRANCIS: I've got one of those already. I don't need two do I?

RACHEL: How come you already have a letter of authorisation?

FRANCIS: *(Aside.)* This is trickier than I thought. *(FRANCIS takes the letter.)*

You're right. I'm gonna need that.

RACHEL: And any letters you collect are private. Is that clear?

FRANCIS: Don't worry guvnor, I won't even read them myself.

RACHEL: I'm gonna have a couple of beers, and a lie down in my room. *(RACHEL goes in.)*

FRANCIS: *(Aside.)* You got to concentrate ain't ya, with two jobs. Kaw! I can do it, long as I don't get confused. But I get confused easily. I don't get confused that easily. Yes I do. I'm my own worst enemy. Stop being negative. I'm not being negative. I'm being realistic. I'll screw it up. I always do. Who screws it up? You, you're the role model for village idiots everywhere. Me?! You're nothing without me. You're the cock up! Don't call *me* a cock up, you cock up!

(He slaps himself.) You slapped me!? Yeah, I did. And I'm glad I did. *(He punches himself back.)* That hurt. Good. You started it.

A fight breaks out, where he ends up on the floor. Enter ALAN.

ALAN: What is my life? Am I to eat, drink, sleep, get a good job, marry, honeymoon, have kids, watch them grow up and have kids of their own, divorce, meet someone else, get old, and die happy in my sleep like every other inhabitant of Brighton and Hove? What kind of a life is that? No. I am an artist. Character is action. I cannot allow this late suitor to come along and end my beautiful dream, like a dead, discarded Russian astronaut dog landing on my head. *(He notices FRANCIS.)* My rival's lackey. This will be the beginning of the end.

(To FRANCIS.) Where is the dog, your *guvnor?* He will die today.

ALAN takes his jacket off, rolls his sleeves up, takes his watch off as if preparing for a fist fight.

FRANCIS: Do yourself a favour mate, walk away.

ALAN: You have obviously never been in love.

FRANCIS: *(Counting on his fingers.)* Janice Carter, one; Pamela Costello, two; her gran, three –

ALAN: – bring the cur out here, now!

FRANCIS: You want to talk to my guvnor.

ALAN: Talk a little, yes, and then slaughter a lot.

FRANCIS: Alright, stay there, I'll go and get him. *(FRANCIS heads for the pub door. Just as he gets there STANLEY opens it.)*

STANLEY: Have you been to the Post Office yet?

FRANCIS: I was –

STANLEY: – Who's he?

FRANCIS: He wants a word with my guvnor.

STANLEY: I'm your guvnor.

FRANCIS: Yes. You are aren't you.

STANLEY: He wants a word with me, does he?

FRANCIS: *(Introducing STANLEY to ALAN.)* This gentleman is called Alan.

STANLEY: Oh bad luck.

FRANCIS: I'll be at the post office *(FRANCIS tiptoes backwards out the way, unseen.)*

STANLEY: Are you an actor?

ALAN: Does it show?

STANLEY: The way you stand, at an angle. As if there's an audience, over there.

ALAN: My rival in love, Roscoe Crabbe, arrived from London today and is staying here.

STANLEY: *(Aside.)* Bizarre! Roscoe Crabbe is the name of the chap I killed accidentally last Saturday evening, stabbing him three times in the chest with a knife I'd bought earlier.

ALAN: He has today claimed my bride, my love, my life.

STANLEY: No! Roscoe Crabbe is dead. I know he's dead because a friend of mine knows someone, who's dad works with a chap who says he murdered him.

ALAN: I met him not an hour ago. He lives, his every breath tortures me.

STANLEY: *(Aside.)* I suppose when I fled the club he wasn't actually yet dead. Oh Jeez! If Roscoe did survive and is in Brighton, he's here for one reason only, to kill me. Oh my God.

(To ALAN.) He's not staying here. I know him. I would have seen him.

ALAN: Oh. I was led to believe. No matter. My card. If you see him tell him that his life will only be spared if he gives up his wedding plans.

ALAN gives him a card.

STANLEY: You said your name was Alan? This card says *Orlando* Dangle.

ALAN: Actors' Equity already had an Orlando Dangle.

STANLEY: You *chose* "Alan"?

ALAN: It's 1963, there's a bloody revolution in the theatre and angry young men are writing plays about Alans. What's your name sir?

STANLEY: My name? *(Aside.)* Buggerello! Gonna have to be creative now. Not my best game! *(STANLEY looks at the trash can.)*

Trash can, bench, door, dorian, Dorian!

He looks around again, at the pub sign.

Dorian Pubsign.

ALAN: Pubsign?

STANLEY: Pubsign. It's an old Anglo Saxon guild name. The Bakers baked bread, the Smiths were the blacksmiths, the Pubsigns. Yup! We made the pub signs.

ALAN: It has been a pleasure meeting you Mister Pubsign. *(ALAN exits.)*

STANLEY: Roscoe is in Brighton! I'd be better off lying low in London, than lying low in Brighton. Poor dear Rachel must be terrified. My God! Can this be happening. What to do?! I must go to London, find Rachel. Damn it! I can't! I have to wait here for Rachel's letter.

Enter a POLICEMAN.

Uurgh! Rozzer! *(To the POLICEMAN.)* Lovely day for it!

POLICEMAN: Lovely day for what sir?

STANLEY: Fighting crime.

STANLEY backs into the pub. The POLICEMAN walks on, though he is suspicious. Enter FRANCIS. FRANCIS starts going through the letters of which there are four in all, two letters, and two authorisations. Bit of a routine needed here, with four letters, and pockets etc.

FRANCIS: Authorisation letter. Let's put that in this pocket. Rachel Crabbe. Let's put that in this pocket for now. I'm good at this. I could work for the Post Office. That'd be three jobs. Authorisation. That goes in the authorisations pocket. Stanley Stubbers. *(Puts it in his mouth. Chews a little. Mumbling.)* Don't really need these authorisation letters any more do I? *(He puts the authorisations in the same pocket as the Rachel letter.)*

So this pocket is now for Stanley Stubbers' letters. Good. What are these then? I'm getting confused now. Two authorisation letters. If there's two letters they definitely need their own pocket. What's this? Stanley Stubbers. That's the one that tasted quite good.

Puts it in his mouth. Chews a little more.

Mm.

He takes a proper bite.

Not bad for paper. Bit dry. Could do with a bit more ink. I didn't know paper could taste this good. I might go back to communion.

Really eats the letter. STANLEY enters from the pub.

STANLEY: Henshall! Did you get the letters.

FRANCIS: Yes guvnor. Yeah, they're all here.

STANLEY: How many? Just the one I guess.

FRANCIS: Er… Let's have a look. *(He goes through the letters.)*
There's nothing here for you guvnor.

STANLEY: What are those letters then?

FRANCIS: These are…decoy letters.

STANLEY: Decoy letters?

FRANCIS: The Post Office release them like homing pigeons.
They record how many find their way back, and how
many get shot down and run over.

STANLEY grabs him by the ear, and by the balls.

STANLEY: The truth Henshall! Or you'll never bugger the
dolphin again!

FRANCIS: *(In pain.)* These are Paddy's letters.

STANLEY: Paddy?

FRANCIS: An old friend of mine, he was collecting letters
for his boss, but he hadn't had any LUNCH, yet, so I
picked his letters up for him, so he could go and have
HADDOCK AND CHIPS AND MUSHY PEAS!

STANLEY: This letter is for my intended, Rachel Crabbe!

STANLEY releases his grip on FRANCIS' testicles and takes the letters.

FRANCIS: You can't open other people's letters!

STANLEY: Why not?

FRANCIS: It's a very deep human thing that's really basic and
doesn't need explaining.

STANLEY: At boarding school we opened each other's post all
the time.

FRANCIS: Yes, but you also held masturbation relay races.
Which is not normal either?

STANLEY: No?

FRANCIS: No.

STANLEY: Mmm. It felt pretty good at the time. *(STANLEY walks away from FRANCIS to share the contents with the audience.)*

(Aside.) It's from Jackie, Rachel's best friend.

(Reading.) Dear Rachel, The police know you fled to Brighton dressed as a man so The Evening News carried an artist's impression of what you might look like in mens' clothes. You ended up looking a bit like Ringo Starr, who's already been arrested twice. *(Aside.)* Rachel, the woman I love, is in Brighton disguised as the percussionist of a popular beat combo! *(Reading.)* They also carried a boxing photo of Stanley –

(Aside.) – that's me!

(Reading.) It's so awful that you have to go to Australia. Love, Jackie. Three kisses.

(Aside.) Three kisses? That's a bit girls-only-Greek-island.

(To FRANCIS.) Henshall! Have you met Paddy's boss?

FRANCIS: No.

STANLEY: Find Paddy, tell him to tell his employer I'm staying here.

(STANLEY exits into the pub.)

FRANCIS: I'll look for Paddy after LUNCH!

STANLEY: NO! Now! This is a matter of life or death

STANLEY sneaks back into the pub. FRANCIS addresses the audience from the stage.

FRANCIS: Has anyone got a SANDWICH!? *(Beat.)* There's a thousand people here and no one's got a York ham and mustard? Bacon, lettuce, tomato? *(Pleading.)* Cheese? Anyone? What? Has he got one…?

Opportunity to improvise with audience members throwing sandwiches. Enter BARMAN.

BARMAN: – I got a minute, if you want a hand with that trunk of yours.

FRANCIS: Yes, but…

FRANCIS is caught between a sandwich and duty.

BARMAN: Now!

FRANCIS: Alright! Let's do it. Let's get the trunk out of the motor.

He and the barman head off upstage left. Enter RACHEL. The BARMAN sits, upstage, looking at his watch, taking no real interest.

RACHEL: Oi! Francis! Have you got my letters mate?

He hands over the opened letter to RACHEL plus one other.

FRANCIS: There you go guv, none of yours have been eaten. I'm going to get your trunk –

FRANCIS heads off quickly with the BARMAN.

RACHEL: – Oi! Francis! This letter has been opened!

FRANCIS: *(Aside.)* Oh no, I need a convincing excuse here.

(To RACHEL.) I had to open it because I realised that there was a small, distressed frog trapped inside.

(Aside.) Yes! Come on!

RACHEL: How did you know there was a small distressed frog trapped inside a sealed envelope?

FRANCIS: *(Aside.)* Shit! There was no frog, actually. I had a letter for me, which I hadn't yet opened, and I opened yours by mistake.

RACHEL: Get my trunk to my room, then come back here. We need to talk.

(She sits and reads the letter and does not notice the trunk business.) It's from a friend of mine. Jackie. *(She reads it.)* I wish I could talk to Jackie, but she doesn't have a telephone at home. I bet one day, in the future, everyone will have their own telephone that they carry around with

them. Oh God no, it would be hell wouldn't it. Wherever you are your mum might ring. Work. People trying to sell you stuff. It might ring in the theatre. Oh God no, please, don't let it happen it would be hell.

FRANCIS and the BARMAN enter, the BARMAN is carrying the trunk on his own.

FRANCIS: *(To BARMAN.)* …Yeah, it's a condition of the spine, they call it Ankylosin Spondilitis, basically if I lift anything heavier than a knife and fork I go blind.

BARMAN in, and door closed.

RACHEL: Are you stupid?

FRANCIS: No. I could've gone to university, if I'd got the qualifications.

RACHEL: I need a clean shirt. I smell like a smelly horse. What's your ironing like?

FRANCIS: World class. I've got the equivalent of a magna cum laude in ironing from Oxford.

RACHEL: My shirts are in the trunk. Here's the key. *(RACHEL gives FRANCIS the key.)* Has Charlie the Duck been here with the money?

FRANCIS: No.

RACHEL: I better go chase him up. *(Exit RACHEL stage right.)*

FRANCIS: He didn't say the shirts needed ironing urgently. Maybe I could go to the High Street and beg for some food.

FRANCIS heads for the audience but is stopped by CHARLIE.

Enter CHARLIE CLENCH from stage left. He is dressed for the bank and wearing a trilby.

He is carrying a large bulky envelope.

CHARLIE: Is your guvnor in? I've got his bangers here.

FRANCIS: His sausages?

CHARLIE: Bangers and mash.

FRANCIS does a look to the audience as if to say my prayers have been answered.

FRANCIS: *(Aside.)* Sausage and mash in an envelope?! I've just seen the future.

CHARLIE: It's cockney rhyming slang. Bangers and mash – Cash.

FRANCIS: Agh! It's not food then?!

CHARLIE: It's two hundred pounds for your guvnor. Don't let me down.

FRANCIS: WHEN AM I GOING TO EAT!

CHARLIE exits. Enter STANLEY.

STANLEY: Henshall! Did you find your friend, Paddy?

FRANCIS: Er…I've arranged to meet him later, on the pier.

STANLEY: What's that?

FRANCIS: It's an envelope full of money, for my guvnor.

STANLEY: I'm your guvnor.

FRANCIS: You are, aren't you. Go on, take it. I don't care any more.

STANLEY: Must be that pawn broker down the road. Did he have a hearing aid, a wig, and a glass eye?

FRANCIS: For sale?

STANLEY: No, as functioning parts of his anatomy.

FRANCIS: He was wearing a hat.

STANLEY: Must be him. I left a pocket watch with him, earlier. I like Brighton! Pubs with food, cash delivered, it's a better kind of England!

FRANCIS: I'm going to go in now and get on with your ironing.

STANLEY: Initiative. I like it.

FRANCIS: I thought we'd already agreed I'd iron your shirts.

STANLEY: No. But have a go. I never understood how irons work. I bunked off physics, spent every lesson in the radiation cupboard trying to make my penis glow.

They go in.

End of Scene.

SCENE THREE

CHARLIE CLENCH's house. CHARLIE. PAULINE is crying.

PAULINE: I can't marry that tiny, weird looking, vicious, homosexual, short arsed, runt of a criminal.

CHARLIE: Why not, what you got against him?

PAULINE: I want to marry for love.

CHARLIE: Trust me. You don't wanna marry for love! When your muvver… *(Breaks up slightly.)* …when she left me I… I… *(Breaks up.)* –

PAULINE: – Don't upset yourself, dad. What you tryna say?

CHARLIE: I'm tryna say that love passes through marriage quicker than shit through a small dog.

PAULINE: But I love Alan.

CHARLIE: Marry Roscoe and you get a detached house in Essex. In the forest. A mile long drive.

PAULINE: From where?

CHARLIE: From the nearest public thoroughfare! He won't ever touch you. You just gotta go to the boxing on his arm, show the world he ain't homosexual, and at two thousand a year he's paying you more than John Lennon's earning.

PAULINE: I didn't know he was living with John Lennon?

CHARLIE: *(Aside.)* They've tried, but they can't make bricks thicker.

Five years ago, you agreed to this agreement.

PAULINE: Five years ago I was young and stupid.

CHARLIE: So what's changed?

(DOLLY enters.)

DOLLY: Roscoe's back.

(PAULINE starts wailing. Enter RACHEL.)

CHARLIE: Hello Roscoe! Come in son. Did you get your bangers?

RACHEL: I did not get my bangers, no. And I didn't get no banker's draft neither. That's why I'm here mate.

CHARLIE: I give the bangers to that geezer of yours. The two hundred.

RACHEL: Alright. And the six thousand?

CHARLIE: Let's have lunch, at the Cricketers, I'll have it all signed off by then.

RACHEL: What's she singing about?

CHARLIE: This is her grieving for your death from three days ago. She's always a bit behind.

RACHEL: I'd like a word with her, if that's alright. Alone.

CHARLIE: Alright Roscoe. Take your time.

(CHARLIE exits.)

RACHEL: Pauline –

PAULINE: – Piss off! I hate you! You've ruined my life.

RACHEL: I know what would make you feel better.

PAULINE: You bleeding well touch me, and I'll scream!

RACHEL: I have a secret.

PAULINE: I don't want to know anything about your life, I wish you were dead.

RACHEL: *(Aside.)* I can't bear to see her suffer any longer.

I am dead.

PAULINE: Are you? No! Really? What's it like?

RACHEL: Roscoe, my brother is dead.

PAULINE: You're Roscoe's brother?!

RACHEL: Sister.

PAULINE: I don't understand!

RACHEL: I'm Rachel, Roscoe's twin sister.

PAULINE: Oh yeah! They said he was one of two identical twins.

RACHEL: It is not possible for identical twins to be different sexes.

PAULINE: Why not?

RACHEL: Because one would be male and the other female.

PAULINE: I don't understand.

RACHEL: All you need to know is that I am a woman.

PAULINE: So, hang on, that means, I can't marry you, dunnit.

RACHEL: More importantly it means you can marry Alan.

PAULINE: Can I!?

RACHEL: In the near future.

PAULINE: I'd better go tell him.

(PAULINE makes for the door, but RACHEL stops her, grabbing her sleeve.)

RACHEL: No! My identity must remain a secret. I need your help.

PAULINE: I'll do anything to marry Alan. I love him.

RACHEL: I too am in love.

PAULINE: Really? With Alan?

RACHEL: No. His name's Stanley.

PAULINE: It's weird innit. Love. It's like being mad.

RACHEL: Insane. Look at me. Dressed in my dead brother's clothes.

PAULINE: Maybe this is your way of grieving for him.

RACHEL: Yes. I hadn't thought of that. *(They hold hands, consoling each other.)*

We girls have to help each other.

They hug spontaneously. Enter CHARLIE.

CHARLIE: Sorry, shoulda knocked. Well, well I never. I'll come back in half an hour. Put a record on. *(CHARLIE turns to go.)*

RACHEL: Charlie, you can go ahead with plans for our wedding.

CHARLIE: Right!?

PAULINE: But I need time…to choose a dress.

RACHEL: And the cashier's cheque is –

CHARLIE: – Roscoe, trust me, the money's no problem. I'd better go tell Laurence Olivier it's definitely off. Kaw! Harry Dangle won't like this. *(CHARLIE heads for the door and is gone.)*

PAULINE: Oh bloody heck! What if dad tells Alan, Alan might think we've had it off.

RACHEL: What would Alan do, if he were to think that?

PAULINE: He'd go into one. He's known as a dangerous actor.

RACHEL: I can look after myself.

PAULINE: I know, but still, I'd better get to him before dad does.

(PAULINE heads for the door. But is held by the arm by RACHEL.)

RACHEL: You swore to keep my secret.

PAULINE: How long do I have to go along wiv this lie?

RACHEL: Stanley and I are going to have to live in Australia.

PAULINE: Oh no! Australia?! Oh no! Oh my God! Australia? Uurgh! How awful!

RACHEL: It'll be a terrible outdoorsie life, sustained by lager, barbecues, and opera.

PAULINE: I sympathise wiv yer, but my Alan, he's suffering right now.

RACHEL: Trust me. My plan will deliver to you the husband of your choice –

PAULINE: – Alan?

RACHEL: Yes, Alan. And the pain you feel now, will be forgotten in a couple of weeks' time. The night always seems darkest just before dawn.

PAULINE: What?

RACHEL: That bit of the night, you know, just before dawn always seems really dark, although it isn't, it's just the contrast with the light of morning.

PAULINE: I don't understand!

End of Scene.

SCENE FOUR

A first floor aperitif bar squeezed between two private dining rooms. The dining rooms are named the Compton Room (stage right) and the Bradman Room (stage left). They both have photographs of the heroes fixed to the door or above the door. Upstage centre the stairs go down to the ground floor and the kitchens. There are autographed cricket bats on the wall. Upstage left is a life sized plywood cut-out representation of

W.G. Grace with the face cut away. FRANCIS enters from the stairs, in a panic. Goes to the door of the Compton suite.

FRANCIS: Roscoe, has insisted on having lunch with Charlie, up here, in private, instead of downstairs in the bar. Don't ask me why he wants to eat in private. I'm not paid to think. Mr Stubbers is having a lie down, which I guess you have to do a lot of when you're *lying low.* I've been nil by mouth for sixteen hours. I'm only alive cos me gall bladder's worked out a way of eating me kidneys. But! The good news is it's lunch time. There's gonna be food everywhere, and all I've got to do is organise a stash, you know, leftovers, the odd whole course going missing. Hide it under here maybe. *(He looks under the table. Comes up with a mousetrap.)*

A mousetrap with a chunk of CHESHIRE CHEESE! My favourite. All white and crumbly. And this bit's only slightly nibbled. *(He licks the cheese with an extended tongue. Enter STANLEY.)*

STANLEY: Henshall!

FRANCIS jumps in fright, the mousetrap goes off on his tongue. He takes the trap off his tongue.

FRANCIS: Aaaargh!

STANLEY: How come a mousetrap went off on your tongue?

FRANCIS: It's a personal thing guv.

STANLEY: Understand! I too enjoy pain. Have you found Paddy?

FRANCIS: I've arranged to meet him after LUNCH.

STANLEY: I've got no time to waste on lunch. I'm going down to the pier to look for him myself.

FRANCIS: *(Aside.)* Now this suits me! Get this guvnor out the way while I serve the other one.

STANLEY: By the way, what does Paddy look like?

FRANCIS: He's a big lad, smells of horses.

STANLEY: Smells *of* horses? Or smells *like a* horse? The former is respectable and an indication of family money, the latter is just poor hygiene.

FRANCIS: At the end of the day, it's the same thing ain't it.

STANLEY: *(A mini epiphany.)* Good point.

FRANCIS: Now take your time guv. There's two piers, I can't remember which pier he said now. Do you want me to order food for you, for later?

STANLEY: Order what you like. When I dine I need to eat in private, waited on by you and you alone. What's this Don Bradman room like? *(He looks into Bradman room.)* Perfect. I'll eat in there. *(Takes out envelope of money.)* I don't want to take all this cash with me. Can I trust you with it Henshall?

FRANCIS: Is it edible?

STANLEY: I doubt it.

FRANCIS: It's safe with me then guv.

STANLEY: I'll slip out the back.

STANLEY slopes off down the service stairs. Enter GARETH and ALFIE. GARETH is thirty something, and a trained head waiter type. ALFIE is meant to be old, slow and doddery.

GARETH: My name's Gareth. I'm the head waiter. This is Alfie.

ALFIE: I'm eighty-six.

GARETH: No you're not. You're eighty-seven.

ALFIE: I thought I was eighty-six.

GARETH: No. That was last year. Be patient with Alfie please, he's a bit deaf, so don't turn your back, he's gonna lip read.

ALFIE: I ain't never going back there! *(To FRANCIS.)* It was a bloody massacre.

GARETH: During the first world war he was at Gallipoli. He has balance problems, he suffers from the tremors, and he's got one of them new fangled pacemakers for his heart.

FRANCIS: Is that all I need to know?

GARETH: One other thing.

FRANCIS: What's that?

GARETH: It's his first day. I've been told to set places for Mr Clench and your guvnor.

FRANCIS: In there, the Compton room, and my other guvnor will eat alone in the Bradman room later, and they've both insisted that I personally wait on their tables.

GARETH: *(Impressed.)* You've got two employers?

FRANCIS: Yeah. I'm that good. I was trained by the legendary French waiter, Jean Jacques Jim.

GARETH: In France?

FRANCIS: Of course.

GARETH: Which town?

FRANCIS: Ashby-de-la-Zouch.

GARETH: That's in Leicestershire.

FRANCIS: It is now.

ALFIE: Do these guvnors of yours know you've got two jobs?

FRANCIS: No, that is our secret for today.

GARETH: What's in it for me and Alfie?

FRANCIS: It's less work for you and you still get paid.

GARETH: What about our tips?

FRANCIS: You'll get a pound each from me at the end of the afternoon.

GARETH: Deal! Alfie! Set one place in the Bradman room. I'll get some wine lists.

ALFIE starts walking towards the Bradman room, very slowly. Off go the waiters into their respective rooms. Enter LLOYD with menu.

LLOYD: How many courses do you think Roscoe and Charlie will want?

FRANCIS: Seven.

LLOYD: Seven. À la carte?

FRANCIS: No! They're gonna eat indoors. I'll order for them.

LLOYD: The menu is in French. How many languages do you speak?

FRANCIS: I speak two languages actually. English *and* French. The menu, por favor.

LLOYD: Por favor is Spanish.

FRANCIS: *(Aside.)* Bloody hell! I can speak three languages.

FRANCIS is given the menu. He spends a couple of beats looking at it, frowning, sweating.

LLOYD: Alfie!

FRANCIS: He's in the Bradman.

LLOYD: Oh. He'll need a menu then. *(LLOYD goes to the threshold of the Bradman suite.)* Alfie! *(ALFIE is in the doorway.)* Jesus! Put this menu and wine list on the table. *(LLOYD gives ALFIE a menu and wine list.)*

(To FRANCIS.) Are you ready to order then?

FRANCIS: *(Closing the menu with a snap)* Yes! Can I have a lot of hot food, and, you know, just keep it coming.

LLOYD: My pleasure.

Exit LLOYD down the stairs. Enter GARETH from the Compton.

FRANCIS: So, Gareth. Alfie! Bring the food to here, this table, and I'll serve it.

GARETH: Alright. Alfie, bring the soup to here. *(ALFIE exits.)*

Enter CHARLIE and RACHEL. FRANCIS puts a finger to his lips to inform the waiters.

Exit GARETH.

RACHEL: What makes me a successful businessman Charlie?

CHARLIE: Your well-known propensity for sickening violence.

RACHEL: Exactly. You ain't got the money have you Charlie?

CHARLIE: This is my problem, I'll have its arse slapped by three o'clock. *And*, I'm paying for lunch, I insist.

RACHEL: Francis! Charlie said he gave you some cash earlier. In an envelope.

FRANCIS: *(Aside.)* Oh no! I can see what's going to happen! Roscoe's gonna take Mister Stubbers's money! That's a disaster! No, wait, it is Roscoe's money. Yes!

(To RACHEL.) There you go. *(Hands it over.)*

I've set two places in here, the Dennis Compton Room.

CHARLIE: *(Panicking.)* I can't eat in there!

RACHEL: Why not?

CHARLIE: When Jean, *(Breaking up.)* when she left me, she ran off with a geezer called Dennis Compton.

RACHEL: Dennis Compton, the famous English cricketer?

CHARLIE: No, he was a driving instructor. But he was called Dennis Compton, so I can't eat in there, I wouldn't be able to keep me food down.

RACHEL: Alright mate. Let's eat in the Bradman room then.

FRANCIS: NO!!!

RACHEL: Why not?

FRANCIS: The gentleman from room ten has already booked this room.

RACHEL: He's not here is he. When room ten arrives, he can have the Compton room. You got anything against the Aussies Charlie?

CHARLIE: No. As it happens, I quite like opera. *(CHARLIE strides into the Bradman room, RACHEL follows and closes the door.)*

FRANCIS: *(Aside.)* Oh shit!

(Enter ALFIE slowly up the stairs with the soup, shaking, and looking like he might lose his balance as he goes.)

FRANCIS: Come on Alfie you can do it!?

ALFIE: This soup must be made of lead, it's bloody heavy.

(He gets to the top, still struggling with his balance. Tureen of soup on a tray.)

FRANCIS: Let me help, I'll take that.

FRANCIS lifts the tureen off the tray. This overbalances ALFIE and he tumbles backwards down the stairs unnoticed by FRANCIS. FRANCIS heads to the Bradman room and has his hand on the door handle when STANLEY opens the upstage right door from the bedrooms, and sneaks in.

STANLEY: Henshall!

FRANCIS: Guv?! You're back, that was quick.

STANLEY: *(Aside.)* I went round to the Palace Pier, couldn't find anyone who smelt like a horse, and the other pier was on fire. Truth is, Brighton is swarming with rozzers.

(To FRANCIS.) I'll eat now.

FRANCIS: Now!?

STANLEY: Yes. Now. What have you got there?

FRANCIS: Your soup.

STANLEY: But I wasn't even here yet.

FRANCIS: That's how good I am.

(STANLEY strides towards the door of the Bradman room.)

FRANCIS: Change of plan guv. You're actually in that room there. The Compton Room.

STANLEY: Why's that?

FRANCIS: There's a honeymoon couple in here.

STANLEY: Really?

FRANCIS: A doctor and nurse, they met in Africa.

STANLEY: *(Aside.)* A Harlequin Romance by Danielle Steel. *The Hospital in Buwambo!*

Bring that soup in, I'm starving, I could eat my own pants.

FRANCIS: *(Aside.)* Oh no! What am I gonna do?!

FRANCIS thinks, then starts heading for the Compton Room door with the soup. He opens the door, and just as he does that RACHEL opens the Bradman door. FRANCIS spins, slams the Compton shut, pressing his body against the Compton door.

STANLEY walks into the Compton Room and closes the door. RACHEL opens the door from the Bradman and collects cutlery and soup spoons from the table. ALFIE starts heading up the stairs slowly with the charcuterie plate.

RACHEL: Oi! Francis, there's only one place setting in here. What you got there?

FRANCIS: Your soup.

RACHEL: Giss it here then. What's the matter wiv you?

Bradman door is closed. We see ALFIE climbing the stairs. FRANCIS comes out of the Compton.

FRANCIS: I haven't eaten for sixteen hours! *(Enter GARETH with water jug.)*

Gareth! I've got two guvnors, two rooms, I need more of everything. Now! Quick.

Enter ALFIE with the charcuterie plate.

ALFIE: *(Panting, out of breath.)* Here's your cold meats.

ALFIE hands over the plate to FRANCIS and then turns up his pacemaker.

FRANCIS: Over here Alfie. *(ALFIE heads for the Compton.)*

Look at that! Beautiful. Ham, beef, what do they call that sliced sausage there?

ALFIE: Pepperonly.

(FRANCIS takes the charcuterie plate from ALFIE and eats a slice. ALFIE watches him.)

FRANCIS: Beautiful.

ALFIE: Sliced donkey.

FRANCIS: I like a bit of donkey. You sound out of breath Alfie?

ALFIE: Them stairs, they tek out of yer. I'll turn mi pace mekker up a couple of notches.

(FRANCIS takes the plate. STANLEY opens the door quickly, knocking ALFIE in the face and over which turns into a roll, and he rolls backwards down the stairs, unseen by STANLEY.)

STANLEY: Where's that soup you had?

FRANCIS: It was cold. I sent it back.

STANLEY: Vichyssoise?

FRANCIS: No. Back downstairs.

STANLEY: Get me the wine list would you.

STANLEY takes the charcuterie plate, and closes the door. Enter GARETH with a second soup tureen.

GARETH: Rule number one, for a waiter. Don't eat the food. Soup for your other guvnor.

FRANCIS: Smashing. And he wants a wine list.

(GARETH reaches out to a supply of wine lists.)

GARETH: Next up is your quenelles de volaille.

FRANCIS: Ah! My favourite, my gran used to cook quenelles de volaille every Christmas Eve.

GARETH: Chicken balls! *(Exit GARETH, with an imperious glare.)*

FRANCIS: Chicken balls. Really? I didn't think chickens had… Cockerels obviously. Never understood soup. You don't need a knife and fork to eat it, so it's not food, so it must be drink, in which case I'd rather have a pint.

He picks up the tureen and drinks the soup straight from the tureen, downs it in one. Ends with a satisfying sigh. Enter RACHEL. FRANCIS hides the empty tureen behind his back.

RACHEL: Francis!

FRANCIS: *(Spitting out soup.)* Yes guv.

RACHEL: Can you clear our table please of the soup, and we'd like to order some wine.

Exit RACHEL into Bradman followed by FRANCIS. FRANCIS returns immediately with their soup tureen and empty bowls. He closes the Bradman door. STANLEY enters from the Compton room and collects a wine menu from the table and returns.

STANLEY: Service! Henshall!

(Seeing no FRANCIS, he picks up the soup and wine list. Turns a page, it's a decent list.) Mmm. Spoke too soon. Winerama!

STANLEY returns to the Compton. Enter FRANCIS from Bradman with their soup tureen and empty bowls. He closes the Bradman door.

FRANCIS: Yes! There's some soup left in here. I need someone to look after this soup for me. *(He goes into the front row, and hands the tureen to KATHRYN, a plant.)* What's your name?

KATHRYN: Kathryn O'Connor.

FRANCIS: Kathryn O'Connor. Thanks for giving us all the information! Do you want to give out your social security number as well? Will you look after this soup? Hide it under your seat. Thank you Kathryn O'Connor. Don't let any of these bastards touch it. *(FRANCIS is back on stage. ALFIE arrives with the chicken balls.)* What you got there Alfie?

ALFIE: Chicken balls.

FRANCIS: Thank God they're not donkeys. How many have we got here?

ALFIE: Twelve.

FRANCIS: Right. Three plates. *(ALFIE gives him three plates. FRANCIS dishes up four chicken balls to each plate, then eats one chicken ball with each reasoning, leaving only one chicken ball on each of the plates.)* Three diners, so that's four each and none for me, or three each and three for me.

ALFIE: 'kin 'ell! He's eating the 'kin chicken balls!

FRANCIS: Or two each and six for me.

ALFIE: Eh! You can't do that son. They're not for you. What they like?

FRANCIS: Beautiful. Or one each and nine for me. *(He picks up two plates.)* I'll give these to Roscoe and Charlie. Alfie! You get on that door. Don't let him open the door!

ALFIE walks slowly to the Compton door, FRANCIS sees this and carries ALFIE to speed the process up. FRANCIS heads for the Bradman with two plates.

FRANCIS: I love chicken balls. Succulent. Meaty. Ballsey.

STANLEY enters from the Compton Room.

ALFIE: Sorry.

STANLEY: Henshall, I'll have a bottle of... What are you doing?

FRANCIS: Bringing you your chicken balls guv.

STANLEY: One at a time? You're a strange planet.

FRANCIS: Lloyd is a stickler for presentation.

STANLEY: I want a bottle of the Châteauneuf-du-Pape.

FRANCIS: Right you are Guv.

STANLEY goes back into his room closing the door himself. Enter GARETH with a range of vegetables which he puts on the table.

GARETH: Here are your vegetables.

FRANCIS: He wants a bottle of the Châteauneuf-du-Pape.

GARETH: Certainly.

RACHEL: Francis!

Enter RACHEL.

FRANCIS: Chicken balls guvnor.

RACHEL: About time. *(To GARETH.)* Ah, are you the wine waiter mate?

GARETH: I can be.

RACHEL: Gissa bottle of the 58 Claret.

GARETH: So that's one bottle of Châteauneuf-de-Pape and a bottle of the Claret.

RACHEL: No. Just one bottle of Claret. Alright?

GARETH: Ah yes, my mistake.

RACHEL closes the door.

FRANCIS: Gareth, a word. *(FRANCIS knees him in the balls. He collapses.)* You're lucky, I nearly had to kill you then.

GARETH: Sorry. Not easy is it. Having two bosses.

FRANCIS: Thank you. *(Exit GARETH.)* Now, wow! Look at all these beautiful vegetables. I want some of these for later. *(He eats a few potatoes etc.)* Kathryn O'Connor! I could do with some help.

Come on. *(KATHRYN goes up on stage FRANCIS puts vegetables into the tureen as soon as he can.)* Kaw! That's a lovely dress Kathryn Patterson! Is it made of soup resistant material?

She holds the tureen as FRANCIS fill it with vegetables.

Kathryn! I'm just going to load this up with vegetables for later. Let's get you and the tureen back down there.

LLOYD: Service!

FRANCIS: *(KATHRYN picks up the tureen.)* Hang on!? *(LLOYD begins to climb the stairs in full chef gear.)* Oh bloody hell, Lloyd's coming. You're gonna have to hide Kathryn! Get behind the cricketer. That's it. Step up. Watch the step.

KATHRYN hides behind the W. G. Grace cut-out, she is still holding the tureen. Her face and eyes showing through. It is important that the actress playing KATHRYN behaves like a member of the public would so, for example, she does not speak loudly or place her head perfectly in the hole etc. LLOYD enters carrying a dish with three baked trout in almonds.

LLOYD: This is my dish of the day. Truite aux amandes. Truite?

FRANCIS: Fish.

LLOYD: Trout. Aux?

FRANCIS: *(Musical theatre style.)* Trout Oh!?!

LLOYD: Trout *in.* Amandes?

FRANCIS: I know this one. Germany. Trout in Germany.

LLOYD: Trout in… Germany is Allemanges. Amandes is Almonds.

FRANCIS: Trout in almonds! Yes!

LLOYD: *(Looking to the Compton.)* Where's Gareth? *(LLOYD exits.)*

FRANCIS: For in there? … I'll tell him. I want some of this. I want all of this. Kathryn! Kathryn! *(KATHRYN comes forward. He cuts the head off one of them and puts the body in his stash. He does the same for the other two. He is left with three fish heads.)*

I got it.

He puts each separated fish head on its own plate and puts some almonds on top.

Fish heads in almonds.

He cuts a second head off, puts it on a plate.

They'll think it's posh food won't they. Won't they? It's best you don't get involved. OK Kathryn I'm going to serve these to Roscoe and Charlie. You watch that door. Do not let him open it. *(FRANCIS closes the door.)*

KATHRYN is left for an unbearable amount of time on her own on stage.

FRANCIS rushes out, closes Bradman door, picks up a fish head plate, and starts heading for the Bradman.

FRANCIS: They like you Kathryn! Say something funny!

FRANCIS goes into the Compton suite with one plate. KATHRYN sees ALFIE coming up the stairs. FRANCIS enters from the Compton and sees ALFIE.

FRANCIS: It's Alfie! Hide. Hide Kathryn. Hide! Put your head through the hole this time, that's what it's there for.

FRANCIS comes out of Compton, sees ALFIE, grabs KATHRYN and pushes her back behind the W.G. Grace. Then seeing the stash on the table, panics, and carries it to her as she stands behind W.G..

ALFIE: Got yer wine here son.

FRANCIS: Lovely, can you open that one for me. I'm a bit busy.

ALFIE: Corkscrew?

FRANCIS takes vegetables and wine into the Bradman.

FRANCIS: Vegetables and wine Sir.

ALFIE looks around for a corkscrew.

ALFIE: Corkscrew? Corkscrew.

ALFIE finds a corkscrew, comes downstage and starts to open the Pape but we see him not having the strength to pull open the cork. He eventually bends down, puts the bottle between his feet, and pulls up. Nothing. He looks at the bottle and this time he holds the bottle, stands on the two handle of the cork screw and tries to pull up. Again nothing. He studies the bottle again and pulls at it with his hand. This time the cork releases and he knocks himself out. FRANCIS comes out of the Bradman, sees ALFIE spark out on the floor.

FRANCIS: Kathryn! I leave you on your own for two minutes! What happened?

KATHRYN: I think he banged his head.

FRANCIS: Banged his head? Why didn't you help him then?

STANLEY opens the door of the Compton and KATHRYN hides back behind W.G..

STANLEY: – Henshall! Where's my – *(He stands over the body.)*

(Aside.) Good God! Colonel Mustard in the ballroom with the lead pipe.

And there's my wine. That's Grand Cru. Can't spill that. What a waste. Is this one dead? *(He picks the wine up.)*

FRANCIS: He's got a pacemaker. I suppose I could just turn it up a notch see what happens.

FRANCIS turns and fiddles with the pacemaker dial. ALFIE leaps up and starts tearing around the room at an incredible pace.

FRANCIS: Stop him! Trip him up!

ALFIE bangs into the Bradman door and runs off. RACHEL opens the Bradman and looks out, FRANCIS runs to door and pushes RACHEL back in and slams door shut.

RACHEL: Francis!

STANLEY picks an autographed cricket bat off the wall and whacks him in the face. Which renders him unconscious again. STANLEY goes into his room. FRANCIS kneels beside ALFIE. GARETH is climbing the stairs carrying a crown of lamb, which he sets on the carvery trolley.

GARETH: What's happened to Alfie?

FRANCIS: His pacemaker packed up I think.

GARETH: Let me have a go.

GARETH kneels and fiddles with the pacemaker.

Should be set on three. How come he had it on nine?

FRANCIS: For the stairs.

ALFIE wakes up. And gets up.

GARETH: There you go.

ALFIE: Morning!

GARETH: Morning Alf.

ALFIE: Lovely day for it. Francis, son, don't let the bastards grind you down.

ALFIE heads off downstairs perfectly normally.

GARETH: That's Carré d'agneau. Crown of Lamb. *(GARETH exits.)*

FRANCIS: Oh, look at this Kathryn O'Connor! Lamb chops. Where's the stash!? Come on!

KATHRYN appears with the tureen. FRANCIS separates three chops and puts the remainder in the tureen.

RACHEL: *(Off.)* Francis!

FRANCIS: Kathryn get back behind the cricketer! *(RACHEL appears.)* Yes guv…your lamb chops, à la trolley, carved at the table

RACHEL goes back into the Bradman, as FRANCIS heads for the Bradman with the trolley, just as STANLEY opens the Compton door. FRANCIS slams the Bradman door shut and spins around.

STANLEY: Henshall!

FRANCIS: Yes guv! Lamb on wheels, carved up as you watch by the table.

STANLEY heads back into the Compton followed by FRANCIS. On the threshold of the Compton RACHEL opens the Bradman door.

RACHEL: Francis! I thought you were behind me.

FRANCIS kicks the Compton room door closed, spins around with the lamb.

FRANCIS: Yes guv! Where did you go. I was right behind you and then…

RACHEL goes back into the Bradman quickly followed by FRANCIS and the trolley. RACHEL closes the door behind him. STANLEY opens the Compton door as ALFIE arrives at the top of the stairs.

STANLEY: Henshall! *(To ALFIE.)* Where's he gone?

ALFIE: Please don't hurt me.

STANLEY bemused walks back into the Compton Room. Closing the door. FRANCIS then comes out the Bradman with the trolley.

FRANCIS: What you got there Alfie?

ALFIE: Roast Potatoes.

FRANCIS: Alright! I'm coming through!

STANLEY: Food Fight!

FRANCIS pushes the trolley towards the Compton picking up ALFIE on the trolley as he goes. STANLEY opens the door and they sweep passed him into the room. Enter GARETH with the crêpe suzette ingredients and equipment. Enter FRANCIS with ALFIE on his back, piggy-back style. FRANCIS unceremoniously dumps ALFIE and he falls down the stairs.

GARETH: Crêpe Suzette. When you were training in Ashby-de-la-Zouch, did they teach you how to do a proper crêpe?

FRANCIS: Yeah. Crêpe, Liqueur, matches, what could possibly go wrong? *(GARETH exits downstairs)* Kathryn. Now! Take this soup off the stage. *(KATHRYN appears from behind the cutout cricketer and comes down to the table.)*

Do you know how to do crêpe suzette? Do you serve it and set fire to it or set fire to it and serve it as it were? You haven't got a clue have you? Let's get you and the stash back down there.

STANLEY: *(Off.)* Henshall!

FRANCIS steps back so that KATHRYN can lean over and pick up the tureen. STANLEY opens the door from the Compton.

FRANCIS: Hide! Get down!

FRANCIS jumps, KATHRYN panics, and FRANCIS coaxes her to hide under the table. She needs a lot of convincing.

STANLEY: Problem! This wine cannot be Grand Cru. Taste that. *(STANLEY gives FRANCIS a glass which FRANCIS downs in one.)* What do you reckon? Is it Pape?

FRANCIS: No. Actually I think it's quite good.

STANLEY: Ah! Crêpe Suzette. Go on then. I love to watch Grand Marnier burning.

Go on. You need more than that man! *(FRANCIS drops the bottle "spilling" liquid onto the tray)* Whoopsy daisy. *(FRANCIS lights the liqueur.)* Look at that beautiful!

Flames shoot up everywhere.

FRANCIS/STANLEY: Fire! Fire!

KATHRYN backs out from under the table. FRANCIS chucks a jug of water over her. STANLEY gets a fire extinguisher and drenches KATHRYN from head to toe with foam. She stands there covered in foam like an iced cake.

FRANCIS: Alright. Ladies and Gentlemen! What I suggest we do is take a fifteen minute interval here. You can have a drink. We're going to fill out some Health and Safety forms. But I did it, didn't I! I served two guvnors, and they're still none the wiser, and most important of all, I get to eat! See you in fifteen minutes. Have a good interval!

Interval.

Act Two

Round the back of CHARLIE CLENCH's house. The trading sign reads – SCRAP METALS or CHARLIE CLENCH scrap metal – and a tag sign reads Ferrous and non-Ferrous, copper and York Stone. ALAN, arrives, determined. He takes out a knife. Enter HARRY DANGLE.

ALAN: Destiny. Destiny. Destiny. What is destiny? If you're a bus, your destiny is the bus station. And if you talk to buses, as I do, they tell you that their destiny is writ deep in their bus-y souls, it is inescapable, it is The Timetable. Buses laugh at love. Ha, ha, ha! Love is fluff, very fluffy fluff, destiny is steel.

DANGLE: Orlando?! What are you doing here?

ALAN: My honour has been fiddled with. I said I would return and take my revenge – *et voila*!

He shows the knife.

DANGLE: Where did you get that knife?

ALAN: Woolworths.

DANGLE: Put it away boy. We, the educated classes, have our own weapons; the law; contract; and my particular specialism – *sesquipedalia verbis.*

ALAN: Words?

DANGLE: Not just words, words a foot and a half long.

ALAN: If *sesquipedalia verbis* fails, if Charlie refuses to allow me to marry Pauline, tell him he will have this to deal with. *(He holds the knife out. ALAN exits. CHARLIE opens his front door.)*

CHARLIE: What?

DANGLE: Have the impediments before Alan's marriage to Pauline been removed as I demanded?

CHARLIE: No. And it ain't my fault. I thought Roscoe was dead.

During DANGLE's next speech CHARLIE tries to interrupt but fails.

DANGLE: Your precocious contract with Roscoe was initiated in order to facilitate a relationship of mutual expediency and as such is antithetical to the Judeo/Christian and common law conception of marriage. The contract's legality is at best ephemeral and in resurrecting it, following Roscoe Crabbe's own miraculous resurrection, is a classic exemplar of Breach of Promise. *Post hoc ergo propter hoc.* [After this, therefore because of this.]

CHARLIE: What you trying to say?

DANGLE: You're up shit creek without a paddle!

CHARLIE: In my world there's a code. It ain't written down, there's no books, but it's a code, like the law. I ain't got no choice, but to abide by it.

DANGLE: On reflection I am not sure that I want my son to dive into the fetid pond that is your family. *(Exit DANGLE.)*

CHARLIE: Yeah, yeah. Pauline's gonna marry Roscoe and that's that. And I'll give you some Latin for a change. *Que Sera Sera! (Exit DANGLE. CHARLIE turns to go back indoors. Enter ALAN.)* Bugger me, it's Errol Flynn!

ALAN: Is it true?

CHARLIE: Yeah, it is true, yeah. What?

ALAN: Is Pauline to marry Roscoe Crabbe?

CHARLIE: That's right. Wait here, I'll get you a presents list.

ALAN draws the knife, nervously, a little embarrassed by its reality.

ALAN: Do not torment me!? I am no longer responsible for my actions, I am dangerous, unpredictable, like a wasp in a shop window.

CHARLIE: Where did you get that knife?

ALAN: Woolworths.

CHARLIE: What you gonna do with it sunshine?

ALAN: Don't push me! I can do it.

CHARLIE: No, you can't. 'Cause this is real, it ain't a play.

ALAN lunges towards CHARLIE, CHARLIE parries the knife bearing arm, they are in a clench with CHARLIE holding the knife arm, CHARLIE falls on to his back. CHARLIE is at the mercy of ALAN, who places the knife against CHARLIE's neck. Enter RACHEL.

RACHEL: Alan?

ALAN: Don't come any nearer Roscoe! I will, I can!

RACHEL: Where did you get that knife?

ALAN: Woolworths!

She takes out a flick knife and flicks it open. It's cool, it's gangland, it's the real thing. She walks up to ALAN and places the point of the knife under his chin.

RACHEL: It ain't the knife that's dangerous mate. It's the owner. Throw that away.

ALAN: No. I came here to kill Charlie.

RACHEL: You don't want to kill Charlie, you want to kill me. But you can't because, in the split second it would take to raise your arm, my knife will be sorting out your tonsils. Or have you had your tonsils removed?

ALAN: No. I've still got them.

Enter PAULINE from the house.

PAULINE: Roscoe! Please, don't kill Alan, he don't mean no harm, he's only acting! Where'd yer – … *(PAULINE, ostentatiously, looks at the knife.)*

ALAN: WOOLWORTHS! ON THE HIGH STREET! HARDWARE AND KITCHENS! *(ALAN, distraught at his own failure to act lets go his knife go. RACHEL kicks it away.)*

RACHEL: I'll spare him, for your sake, *my darling.*

ALAN: Oh.

RACHEL: And I expect you, in return, to do me a favour, that is to respect our secret.

PAULINE: I do. I will.

ALAN stands, the action of which releases CHARLIE, who also stands. DOLLY appears at the window. She's watching and listening.

CHARLIE: Is that it then? 'Cause I've got a cup of tea going cold in there.

PAULINE: Yeah, go indoors dad.

RACHEL: Charlie! It's gone three o'clock and I ain't got my money.

CHARLIE: Go indoors Roscoe. I'll sort it for you.

CHARLIE holds the door open for RACHEL, who enters.

Alan, son. A word.

ALAN turns to CHARLIE. CHARLIE nuts him, ALAN collapses. Exit indoors CHARLIE.

PAULINE: Are you hurt my love?

ALAN: Have you been with him?

PAULINE: Been where?

ALAN: Bed!

PAULINE: No! God! Alan. Really, absolutely no, not ever, never, no.

ALAN: The lady doth protest too much methinks.

PAULINE: I'm a virgin! Still. You know I am.

ALAN: Don't I just.

PAULINE: I'm saving myself for you Alan, for when we're married, when we can do it two or three times a week legally.

She grabs him, he tosses her aside, she falls near the knife.

ALAN: No! I think your shared secret is that you've always loved him. You've bewitched him, like you've bewitched me, with your little prick teases. You play a man like a penny whistle. I loathe you.

PAULINE: I'm gonna go do meself in then. *(PAULINE sees the knife. She picks it up.)*

She holds the knife in both hands and holds it against her heart. Because she's kneeling the idea is that she will fall forward on to the knife to kill herself. It looks as if she might do it.

DOLLY: He's not worth it love. He'd stand there and watch you do it, and not raise a finger. Look at him. You're not the great romantic lover are you? You're a bit of a wanker. Let me give you some advice. Men, they'll do anything to get you into bed. Lie, cheat, buy you a bed. And the tragedy is once they've had you, they'll never want you quite as much ever again.

(Aside.) Don't take notes girls, there's a handout at the end.

(PAULINE throws the knife aside, takes DOLLY's hand and stands.)

PAULINE: *(Tearful.)* I can't believe you woulda let me kill meself. You're heartless. I'm gonna die anyway, 'cause I can't live with this pain. And when I'm dead I want you to know that it'll be you wot killed me. *(PAULINE exits into the house, DOLLY moves to follow but stays listening, surreptitiously.)*

ALAN: Frailty, thy name is woman!

DOLLY: You want to watch your tongue young man, slagging us women off. It's 1963, there's a revolution coming. I predict in twenty years time there'll be a woman in ten Downing Street, yeah, and she won't be doing the washing up. Then you'll see exactly what women can do. You'll see a more just and fair society. The feminine voice of compassion for the poor will be the guiding principle of government, and there'll be an end to foreign wars.

DOLLY closes the door and is gone.

End of scene.

SCENE TWO

The pub forecourt. Mid morning. FRANCIS is sitting enjoying the sun, reading a newspaper, and smoking. He puts the newspaper in his pocket.

FRANCIS: So I've eaten. Now, after a lovely big meal there's a couple of things I just can't resist doing. One is having a little smoke – *(Drag on cigarette. Then he lifts a buttock and farts.)*

And that's the other. Beautiful. Some of you out there, who understand your *commedia dell'arte*, those with a liberal education, your hummus eaters, will know that this play is based on Carlo Goldoni's two-hundred-year-old Italian comedy *A Servant of Two Masters* and you will now be saying to yourselves "if the Harlequin, *that's me*, has now eaten, what will be his motivation in the second act". Has anyone here said that? Perhaps in an attempt to impress a date. No. Good. Nice to know we don't have any dicks in tonight. My character, Francis, has to find a new base motivation to drive his actions in the second half. Your job is to try and work out what that might be.

Enter DOLLY, miniskirt, boobs etc. She doesn't see FRANCIS. FRANCIS leches at her. Makes a mucky, lustful face for himself. Adjusts his tackle.

DOLLY: Pauline's written one letter to Alan today, and one letter for Roscoe.

FRANCIS: Are we going then? Majorca?

DOLLY: *(Aside.)* Oh it's him. I like him.

I've got a letter here for your gaffer. Can I trust you with it?

FRANCIS: "Confidential" is my middle name.

DOLLY: What are your other names?

FRANCIS: Francis… Henshall.

DOLLY: So your full name is *Francis Confidential Henshall?*

FRANCIS: At your service, gorgeous.

DOLLY: *(Aside.)* Calling a woman "gorgeous" is patronising, and chauvinist, obviously, but since I fancy him rotten, and I haven't had a proper workout for a while, I'll forgive him.

(To FRANCIS.) You've got honest eyes.

FRANCIS: Thank you. Baby.

DOLLY: No trouble. Big Boy.

FRANCIS: A friend of mine likes you.

DOLLY: What's his name?

FRANCIS: Paddy.

DOLLY: What's he look like?

FRANCIS: Could be a film star.

DOLLY: Godzilla?

FRANCIS: He's a good looking lad. He's er…big boned.

DOLLY: And how did he get big bones?

FRANCIS: The usual. Nature / nurture.

DOLLY: Partly genetic, partly pies?

FRANCIS: He likes his food, yeah.

DOLLY: Does he prefer eating or making love?

FRANCIS: *(Aside.)* Mmm. Tricky one that, innit.

Would you like to meet him?

DOLLY: I wouldn't want to interrupt him if he's eating.

FRANCIS: I'll go and get him. Stay there. Don't put your glasses on.

FRANCIS enters the inn.

DOLLY: *(Aside.)* I've done a lot worse. We've all done a lot worse haven't we girls? We've all woken up 'the morning after the night' before, taken one look at the sorry state of the bloke lying next to us, and we've all leapt out of bed, sat down and written to Parliament demanding that tequila should be a controlled drug. *(Beat.)* Just me then?

FRANCIS returns from the inn wearing a big green hat, the type they might have had kicking around for St. Patrick's day, maybe wellies too, and a Barbour.

FRANCIS: *(Irish accent.)* Now hello there! I'm Patrick. Me friends call me Paddy and I'm in love with you, I am so.

DOLLY: Are you really?

FRANCIS: Yes, I'm a hopeless case. I'm like a cork, tossed on an ocean of desire.

DOLLY: Is that difficult?

FRANCIS: It's exhausting. There's only so much tossing a man can endure. I grew this rose for you now, I did, so, aye.

DOLLY: That's very sweet of you.

FRANCIS: Any chance of a kiss? *(They kiss.)*

FRANCIS uses the newspaper to cover an erection.

I'd better go now, I tied the horse up in a tow zone.

FRANCIS exits.

DOLLY: He's like a big kid. I've always liked that in a man, immaturity.

FRANCIS returns.

FRANCIS: What do you reckon to Paddy? D'yer like him?

DOLLY: Why can't you, Francis, as Francis, just ask me out for a date?

FRANCIS: I've asked you to go to Spain with me, Majorca.

DOLLY: I can't just go to Majorca with you. We need to go on a date first.

FRANCIS: Alright.

Aside, as a question to a female member of the audience.

What's a good first date from the girl's point of view?

Audience member might say dinner, theatre, whatever. This is an opportunity for improvisation.

No! She's got to feel relaxed, secure, not under pressure. Er…?

(To DOLLY.) Dolly? How about me and you, you know, I was wondering, Saturday, Saturday afternoon, not evening, no pressure, would you like to go on a rabbit shoot?

DOLLY: I think you should *(Use the audience suggestion.)* – thank you – and maybe we can go for dinner afterwards. We could give the relationship a go, see if it's got legs.

FRANCIS: And if it hasn't got legs, and neither of us can stand up, we'll have to find something that both of us can do lying down.

DOLLY: You've got everything worked out haven't you Francis?

FRANCIS: I'm a man. We plan. We don't just walk into things with our eyes closed, doing stuff because it *feeeeels* right, like you women do.

DOLLY: *(Aside.) (A look to the audience.)*

FRANCIS: Everything needs planning. Love is no different from… I dunno, building a new petrol station. You can't build the shop before you've sunk the petrol reservoirs.

DOLLY: Surely you can build the shop before you sink the reservoirs if you don't build the shop directly on top of the reservoirs.

FRANCIS: Uurgh! Look, you're not gonna win this argument 'cause I've actually built a petrol station, and it was crucial that we sank the reservoirs before we built the shop or we would have had to 1) build the shop 2) knock it down 3) sink the reservoirs 4) build the shop. Which might well be how a woman would build a petrol station, and I'm not saying there's anything wrong with that apart from the fact that it's brainless!

DOLLY: I'll tell you how a woman would build a petrol station. She'd make sure there was enough land so that you could factor in a pleasant walk from the pump, to the shop. Maybe lay a bit of a lawn down.

FRANCIS: A lawn!?

DOLLY: With some flowers. And a rockery. And somewhere for the kids to play.

FRANCIS: Kids –

DOLLY: – And a separate toilet block for the women which has three times as many cubicles as the mens'!!

FRANCIS: What do you need all that for, it's a petrol station?

DOLLY: Yes, but it could be a *nice* petrol station!

FRANCIS: Nobody in their right mind wants petrol stations to be nice. It's a bloody petrol station! It's not gonna work is it? Men and women. Me and you.

DOLLY: No.

FRANCIS: That's a shame. 'Cause I really fancy you.

DOLLY: Thank you. I've always wanted to be a sex object.

FRANCIS: It's better than not being a sex object innit?

DOLLY: Uurgh!

FRANCIS: We're supposed to be going to Majorca.

DOLLY: You can't deliver Majorca Francis. You're a loser.

FRANCIS: Who's this letter for again?

DOLLY: Your guvnor. *(He starts to open it.)* Don't open it!

FRANCIS: I have to find out who it's for!

DOLLY: Just give it to your boss.

FRANCIS: IT'S NOT AS EASY AS THAT!

DOLLY: I can't see what the problem –

FRANCIS: LOOK! There's no name on the envelope.

DOLLY: What do you need a name for!?

FRANCIS: BECAUSE …BECAUSE…I CAN'T TELL YOU.
IT'S VERY COMPLICATED AND REALLY YOU
DON'T WANT TO KNOW!

*FRANCIS collapses and starts rocking catatonically. Enter RACHEL
with CHARLIE. They stand and view FRANCIS rocking.*

CHARLIE: What's up Dolly?

DOLLY: No idea.

RACHEL: Francis! What's that!?

DOLLY: It's a letter. For you.

FRANCIS stops rocking suddenly and stands.

FRANCIS: *(To DOLLY.)* WHY DIDN'T YOU JUST SAY IT
WAS FOR ROSCOE!?

*DOLLY collapses dramatically on to the floor, and rocks catatonically.
All an act mirroring FRANCIS' reaction.*

DOLLY: BECAUSE I'M A WOMAN AND I'M REALLY
STUPID, AND I CAN'T BE TRUSTED TO DO
ANYTHING PROPERLY! AAAAAGGHHH! *(She stops
abruptly, stands, brushes herself down.)*

Men.

RACHEL: It's been opened. Francis?

FRANCIS: I'm Francis. Yes?

RACHEL: This is the second private letter you've opened
today. I have no choice, mate, you're sacked.

FRANCIS cries.

DOLLY: No! I opened the letter.

CHARLIE: Come again?!

DOLLY: I'm worried sick about Pauline. So I opened the letter.
And I read it.

RACHEL: I don't believe you.

DOLLY: Test me. On the contents.

CHARLIE: Oh bloody hell!

> *(To RACHEL.)* You can't believe her. She'll be tryna get well in with him. *(To DOLLY.)* I know you, around men.

DOLLY: Wot?! And I don't know you Charlie Clench?! I know how the business works, I know how the money gets cleaned, I know……

CHARLIE: – Yeah, yeah, alright, alright! You're very knowledgeable.

DOLLY: I'm going home.

> *(To FRANCIS.)* Nice to see you Francis. I like your friend, Paddy. He's not an idiot.

> *DOLLY exits.*

FRANCIS: *(Shouted after her.)* I'll get us two tickets for Majorca! I can, I will.

CHARLIE: I'll go and see my mate Dino. Give me ten minutes. Carlotti's Amusements Arcade on the front. He owes me one.

> *CHARLIE exits. RACHEL reads the whole of the letter. FRANCIS tries to slowly sneak away.*

RACHEL: *(To FRANCIS, without looking at him.)* Where are you going?

FRANCIS: Me?

RACHEL: Come here.

> *FRANCIS approaches RACHEL. We see STANLEY open a window.*

> *RACHEL has her back to the pub. RACHEL slaps FRANCIS across the face.*

STANLEY: Who's that hitting my man.

FRANCIS: What d'yer do that for?

RACHEL: What's my name?

FRANCIS: Roscoe Crabbe.

RACHEL: And what have you heard about the Crabbes?

FRANCIS: *(Aside.)* No, no. Don't worry, we're not going there. You don't mess with them.

RACHEL: If you need me, I'm in Carlotti's Amusement Arcade. On the front. What are you going to do?

FRANCIS: I'm gonna do your ironing, then I'm gonna try and find Paddy on the pier, like you said.

RACHEL: Who's Paddy? *(A POLICEMAN enters and watches.)*

FRANCIS: *(Aside.)* Shit.

Paddy is a friend of mine who works as a kind of butler to someone in Brighton and he said he could teach me how to iron a shirt properly so that nobody gets seriously injured.

RACHEL: Good man. *(RACHEL exits.)* Afternoon.

FRANCIS: *(Aside.)* My nerves! *(Enter STANLEY.)*

STANLEY: Henshall?! What's going on? I swear I saw a chap slap you across the chops.

FRANCIS: Yeah, one of the locals.

STANLEY: What had you done?

FRANCIS: I kissed his girlfriend.

STANLEY: Out of the blue you just went up and kissed a chap's girl?

FRANCIS: Yup.

STANLEY: That's a bit Japanese. I'm sorry, I'm on his side. Come here.

FRANCIS: Oh no please guv.

(STANLEY slaps him. The POLICEMAN enters.)

STANLEY: Morning.

POLICEMAN: Afternoon.

STANLEY: I'll give you one hour, to finish my ironing that you
never started, and then I want you to go to the pier and
find Paddy.

(STANLEY exits to the pub. Enter ALFIE, with a coat on and scarf.)

FRANCIS: Alfie! Do you know where there's a Thomas
Cook's?

ALFIE: Of course I know her, she's my wife.

FRANCIS: HAS BRIGHTON GOT A TRAVEL AGENTS?

ALFIE: There's a Thomas Cook's opposite Brighton Pavilion.

FRANCIS: Pick us up a brochure for Majorca. I'll either be
ironing indoors, or down on the pier.

(ALFIE exits, on the errand. FRANCIS sits.)

(Aside.) So, do you see how commedia dell'arte works? In
the first half I'm driven by my animal urges, hunger, but
in this second half, because I've eaten, I am humanised,
civilised, and I can embrace the potentiality of love.
Which, in this version, is expressed as a leg-over in
Majorca.

End of Scene.

SCENE THREE

*The corridor outside rooms 10 and 11. An ironing board, and an iron.
STANLEY's trunk is set to stage right outside his room, room 10, and
the trunk is open. RACHEL's trunk is outside room 11, and the trunk
lid closed.*

FRANCIS: *(Direct address.)* Now, Mister Stubbers is asleep
in number ten. Roscoe's chasing Charlie for the money.
That's Mr Stubbers' shirts done. The plan is to do both
sets of ironing and then go and look for Paddy on the
pier. Yes, I know, Paddy doesn't exist, but that's the kind
of insanity that makes perfect sense when you've got two
jobs. *(FRANCIS pulls out a pile of shirts from RACHEL's trunk*

and drops them on the ironing board. On top of the pile of shirts is a framed photograph.) What's this? Bloody hell! It's a framed photograph of Mister Stubbers. These are Roscoe's shirts. What is my guvnor number one Roscoe doing with a framed photograph of my guvnor number two, Mister Stubbers?

STANLEY: *(Off.)* Henshall! Is there a shirt ready yet?

Enter STANLEY naked from the waist up, but wearing trousers with braces hanging down. The great shock though is that he is extraordinarily hairy. His chest and up to his neck is totally covered in thick chest hair. It is extreme. STANLEY walks downstage of the ironing board and turns upstage showing his back, which is even worse, hairy like a gorilla. FRANCIS is gobsmacked.)

STANLEY: What are you gawping at Henshall? Never seen a man naked from the waist up eh? Don't tell me you're the kind of chap that didn't shower. That's how we won two world wars. The Germans had superior technology, but our officers showered together. This is the business Henshall.

(He picks up the framed photo.) What's that?

FRANCIS: Oh sorry guv, that's mine.

STANLEY: *(Aside.)* This is a framed photograph of me on graduation day, the very one I gave to Rachel. Is it me? Yes, that third class honours degree in Zoology has got my name on it.

(To FRANCIS.) Are you developing a thing for me?

FRANCIS: No guv. It's a nice frame.

STANLEY: Where did you get it?

FRANCIS: *(Aside.)* I've gotta be very careful what I say here.

(To STANLEY.) I bought it off Paddy, who was given it by his previous employer in lieu of payment before…he died.

Silence.

STANLEY: Before he did…before he did what?

FRANCIS: Before he did…die.

STANLEY: He did die did he?

FRANCIS: He did.

STANLEY: What did he die of?

FRANCIS: He was diagnosed with diarrhoea but died of diabetes.

STANLEY: He died of diabetes did he?

FRANCIS: He did didn't he.

STANLEY: Where you there?

FRANCIS: When?

STANLEY: When he was diagnosed with diarrhoea but died of diabetes.

FRANCIS: No, I was in Didcot, and he was diagnosed with diarrhoea but died of diabetes in Dagenham.

STANLEY: When did he die?

FRANCIS: Of diabetes? Or of diarrhoea?

STANLEY: He didn't die of diarrhoea he died of diabetes.

FRANCIS: He did did he? Where?

STANLEY: In Dagenham! Damn it! That's what you said!

FRANCIS: Paddy told me it was a couple of days ago.

STANLEY: Rachel is dead. But she is all I live for. Grief. Grief. Look, I'm shaking. I'm shaking. My girl, my love, my life, is dead. Breathe man, breathe. Everything. There is nothing without her.

STANLEY goes back into his room. The door closes.

FRANCIS: That went quite well. *(FRANCIS continues ironing.)*

CHARLIE: *(Off.)* I'm like you, I prefer cash –

FRANCIS: *(Aside.)* Just my luck! It's my other guvnor, Roscoe, with Mister the Duck.

Enter RACHEL and CHARLIE.

CHARLIE: I'm disappointed in Dino. It's not like Dino to let me down. I'm glad you didn't take his cheque. What's a cheque? A cheque is a promise. And a promise in this modern world is about as much use as a nun's tits.

RACHEL: Charlie!? Please.

RACHEL is visibly shocked, and turns away. CHARLIE is confused. FRANCIS shrugs his shoulders.

CHARLIE: I'm sorry. Did I offend you? I thought we were all men together.

RACHEL: Your failure to deliver means that I will have to change my plans.

CHARLIE: Give me the weekend. I'm playing golf Sunday with –

RACHEL: – shut it! Francis, look in my trunk, find my diary.

FRANCIS asks one specific woman in the audience for help identifying ROSCOE's trunk.

FRANCIS: Oh no! Can you remember which trunk is Roscoe's? This one? Thank you Madam, You are a lifesaver… There you are guvnor.

FRANCIS reaches into STANLEY's trunk and takes out a diary with letters tucked inside, and he hands it over to her.

RACHEL: This is not my diary.

FRANCIS: *(To audience member who "helped" identify trunk.)* Stupid Cow! Ah! Yes, there it is! Kaw! I've been looking for that! It's mine!

He tries to take it off RACHEL but RACHEL hangs on to it.

RACHEL: But you handed it to me, thinking it was mine.

FRANCIS: The reason is… I haven't owned it for very long, so I don't yet recognise it that easily. *(RACHEL moves downstage.)*

RACHEL: *(Aside.)* This diary, is Stanley's. These are the letters in which I express my love for him, letters and diagrams which celebrate the most intimate details of our love making. Oh my God! But how…

(To FRANCIS.) Francis! How come this diary, and these private letters, are in your possession?

FRANCIS: *(Aside.)* I've gotta be very careful what I say here.

(To RACHEL.) I bought it off Paddy.

RACHEL: The ironing expert?

FRANCIS: Yes. Who was given it in lieu of payment, by my previous employer just before he died.

(Aside.) If it ain't broke, don't fix it.

RACHEL is stunned into silence.

RACHEL: He died did he?

FRANCIS: He did.

RACHEL: How did he die?

FRANCIS: He died of disease.

RACHEL: Where?

FRANCIS: Where was the disease, or where did he die of disease?

RACHEL: Where did he die of disease?

FRANCIS: Dorking.

RACHEL: And where was the disease?

FRANCIS: In his diaphragm.

RACHEL: So he died of a disease of the diaphragm in Dorking?

FRANCIS: He did didn't he?

RACHEL: Do you know Dorking?

FRANCIS: I don't. Do you know Dorking Mister Duck?

CHARLIE: Indeed I do. Dorking is directly north of here.

RACHEL: One might pass through Dorking on the way to Brighton?

CHARLIE: If you're daft and don't know what you're doing, definitely.

RACHEL: *(Aside.)* Definitely Stanley.

(Letting her disguise drop now.) Stanley! Dead?! No! My love, dead?! No! This cannot be! Without Stanley my life is nothing. I do not want to live, here, on this earth, alone without him. I have given him my life, my love, my body.

CHARLIE and FRANCIS are confused.

FRANCIS: *(Aside.)* Bloody hell, he's a woman!

CHARLIE: Roscoe? You're not Roscoe, you're Rachel?

RACHEL: Yes. I am in disguise as my twin brother. Who is also dead. I have lost a brother, and the love of my life both in the one week.

CHARLIE: You proper fooled us. I take my hat off to you. I guess it was easy enough 'cause you and Roscoe was identical twins.

RACHEL: Roscoe was a man. I, as you can see, am a woman. So we cannot be identical twins.

CHARLIE: Why not?

RACHEL: – Excuse me gentlemen. I am in mourning. For a brother, and, a husband.

She exits to her room.

CHARLIE: I better go tell Harry Dangle this. His lad'll be chuffed to bits. Unless he's been and gone and done an Hamlet by now.

FRANCIS: What's an Hamlet?

CHARLIE: An Hamlet is when you flip, kill everyone including yourself.

FRANCIS: That's a bit rash.

CHARLIE: Not rash enough. The last time I saw it, it took him five hours.

Exit CHARLIE.

End of Scene.

SCENE FOUR

The pier. Enter STANLEY at pace. He jumps up on to the railing, hanging on to the lamp post. He takes a look at the ocean, and jumps.

STANLEY: No! No! RACHEL!!!

Enter RACHEL, she climbs up on to the pier railing holding on to the lamp post stage right. Enter LLOYD at pace, he stops, believing that advancing might make RACHEL jump.

RACHEL: STANLEY!

LLOYD: What you doin' girl!?

RACHEL: I will Lloyd! I will! Stanley is dead. I love him. He is everything. Without him this life has nothing to offer me.

Enter by climbing up, STANLEY.

STANLEY: Rachel?!

RACHEL: Stanley?!

LLOYD: Mister Pubsign?!

STANLEY: Rachel, my darling, I thought I'd lost you.

RACHEL: I cried Stanley, you don't know how much I cried.

Still perilous on the pier railings.

LLOYD: Don't you think it might be a good idea if you both stepped down from off of that railing there.

STANLEY: Good thinking! *(They both climb down. They hug.)* My little badger!

RACHEL: My hairy bear!

LLOYD: *(Aside.)* My time to go!

LLOYD starts to leave.

RACHEL: Lloyd! Wait. *(RACHEL comes downstage to talk to LLOYD. This is private from STANLEY.)*

I'm pretty certain Paddy is behind this.

LLOYD: Who the hell is Paddy?

RACHEL: He's a friend of Francis, works for Stanley. I need to talk to Francis. Drag his arse down here would you Lloyd?

LLOYD: My pleasure. I can't say no to you. You're like a daughter to me girl!

RACHEL: You're the very best of men Lloyd. Has anyone ever told you that?

LLOYD: Yes. *(LLOYD looks to the audience with a wink.)*

Exit LLOYD. RACHEL and STANLEY are alone. RACHEL runs to STANLEY.

STANLEY: What made you think I was dead badgie?

RACHEL: I was scared, after the fight, and I hired a minder for protection, and he had this – *(She shows STANLEY's diary and her letters.)*

STANLEY: – Bacon and Eggs! That's my private diary!

RACHEL: – and all the love letters I've ever sent you.

STANLEY: No!?

RACHEL: – My minder said he'd bought your diary from a friend of his who had worked for you –

STANLEY: – for me!?

RACHEL: For you. But you'd died, and you'd given him the diary in lieu of payment.

STANLEY: *(Aside/shocked.)* I don't remember doing any of this!

Did he read any of your love letters?

RACHEL: I can't be sure.

STANLEY: Let's hope not eh, one or two of them have got some really good bits.

RACHEL: But what made you think I was dead?

STANLEY: My man had in his possession that framed photograph of me, the one I'd given you.

RACHEL: But how come your man had my photograph of you?

STANLEY: Paddy's story is that you gave it to him on your death bed, so I presumed that you must be Paddy's employer who died. But you're not dead.

RACHEL: Did you feel terrible, hairy bear?

STANLEY: I've never felt worse. I felt like a floral clock in the middle of winter.

RACHEL: *(Beat.)* That's exactly how I felt! All the flowers dead!

STANLEY: And yet the mechanism of the clock is pointlessly turning!?

RACHEL: The hour hand pointing to a dead geranium!

STANLEY: The minute hand stuck on a long gone begonia.

RACHEL: Stanley, I really don't want to go to Australia.

STANLEY: Oh. Thank Christ! I never did. I can't stand bloody opera.

RACHEL: What can we do?

STANLEY: Could you marry a murderer?

RACHEL: I guess, I'm already in love with a murderer.

STANLEY: Who?!

RACHEL: You.

STANLEY: Oh God! Don't do that.

Enter LLOYD dragging FRANCIS along.

81

RACHEL: Here's one of the troublemakers now.

STANLEY: Thank you Lloyd, but in an ideal world, we need them both here. It wouldn't be right to light a fire under one of them, and let the other one get away with it.

LLOYD: He's the only one I've seen.

Enter ALFIE carrying a Thomas Cook's travel brochure.

ALFIE: Here you go son, here's your brochure.

LLOYD: Maybe Alfie would know.

STANLEY: Alfie, have you seen the other gentleman.

ALFIE: There's new toilets at the end of the pier.

RACHEL: HAVE YOU SEEN PADDY?

ALFIE: They had to put newspaper down 'cause I'd had a banana.

FRANCIS: One minute, please?!

FRANCIS takes ALFIE to one side, out of earshot. STANLEY and RACHEL talk together. Hands over travel brochure, FRANCIS takes it, and rapidly finds the section on Majorca.

Now listen, there's a woman called Dolly works for Charlie Clench, the scrap metal dealer. Give her this Majorca page.

FRANCIS gives the Majorca page from the brochure to ALFIE.

ALFIE: How will I recognise this Dolly?

FRANCIS: Easy. *(He mimes big breasts with his hands.)*

ALFIE: She's got arthritic hands?

FRANCIS: No, she's a big girl. Tell Dolly that Paddy is dead, so she'll have to go to Majorca with me.

ALFIE: You ain't got the money son. It's fifty quid a ticket.

FRANCIS: Not yet but I'm working on it.

ALFIE goes to leave but is accosted by LLOYD.

STANLEY: Henshall! I think this Paddy is the cause of all our problems.

FRANCIS: Yes! And I have a completely brilliant plan which will punish him.

STANLEY: Hit me.

FRANCIS: *(To STANLEY.)* There's this sweet, shy, innocent girl called Dolly –

STANLEY: – is she a virgin?

FRANCIS: Definitely

STANLEY: Went out with a virgin once. Not for long, obviously, that'd be stupid.

FRANCIS: Her Paddy has tricked Dolly into going for a dirty weekend in Margate.

STANLEY: What a Country Life!

FRANCIS: But she has this dream of going to Majorca, but she hasn't got the fifty quid for a ticket. If you could buy her a ticket to Spain then she won't want to go to Margate and we would have rescued her from Paddy's evil scheme and punished Paddy at the same time.

STANLEY: Brilliant! Here's fifty, sterling, go to the travel agent get that poor girl a ticket.

FRANCIS: Wait! Do you think we should let her go on her own?

STANLEY: To Spain, no. Not with their men. I wouldn't trust a Spaniard alone with a Hostess Twinkie. When's this dirty weekend?

FRANCIS: Week after next.

STANLEY: Here's another fifty, Henshall. You're just going to have to go with her. And if anything happens between you, at least the cherry was picked by an Englishmen.

STANLEY heads upstage.

FRANCIS: Miss? A word.

RACHEL and FRANCIS go downstage with STANLEY's nodded consent.

RACHEL: We need to punish Paddy. He nearly caused two suicides.

FRANCIS: Mister Stubbers and I, have a plan. Paddy has asked Dolly to go to Kent with him for a dirty weekend, but if I offer Dolly a week in Majorca, she's bound to prefer sunny Spain over forty-eight hours face down, handcuffed to a Margate four poster.

RACHEL: It would certainly be revenge on Paddy and much more satisfying than a punch in the face. What do you need?

FRANCIS: Fifty quid and next week off.

RACHEL: Brilliant, here's fifty.

RACHEL gets out a roll and gives FRANCIS fifty, and goes upstage to join STANLEY.

FRANCIS: *(Aside.)* Yes! One hundred and fifty quid! That's two flights and fifty spenders! I'm a genius.

A POLICE whistle blows offstage. Two uniformed POLICEMEN run on.

STANLEY: Rozzers!

RACHEL: Oh my God! What do we do?

LLOYD: Split up! Meet at Charlie's! Alfie!

They all split up and run off in different directions. ALFIE beats the POLICEMEN up.

End of Scene.

SCENE FIVE

At CHARLIE CLENCH's house. Same as Act One Scene One. The living room. CHARLIE, DOLLY, DANGLE, ALAN and PAULINE. ALAN is kneeling in the centre of the room. PAULINE has her back turned against him, looking out the window.

DOLLY: How long's this gonna take? I should have finished work at six and in an ideal world I'd be home by now relaxing in a hot bath with a fireman.

CHARLIE: *(To PAULINE.)* Come on Pauline, forgive the lad. He made a mistake.

PAULINE: *(With underlying tenderness.)* You've been really really horrible to me recently Alan.

DANGLE: *(To CHARLIE.)* There is tenderness there.

CHARLIE: *(To DANGLE.)* She called him Alan.

ALAN: I would cut myself and offer you my blood but first observe my tears.

ALAN is crying.

CHARLIE: Kaw! Look at that. He can turn it on like a tap! You gotta give it to him aintcha! Amazing! Where's he going again?

DANGLE: The Royal Acadamy of Dramatic Art.

CHARLIE: Turn around girl, you can't miss this, he's actually crying real tears.

PAULINE turns around. DANGLE and CHARLIE nod to each other hopefully.

PAULINE: *(Sigh.)* Don't cry Alan.

DANGLE: *(Under his breath.)* Excellent!

CHARLIE: *(To DANGLE.)* Them tears done the trick!

ALAN: Pauline, will you share my life with me?

DANGLE: *(Under breath.)* Yes!

CHARLIE: *(Under breath.)* Come on girl!

PAULINE: I dunno, you said you loathed me.

DANGLE/CHARLIE: *(Deflating.)* Oh! / Shit!

ALAN: I did loathe you, yes. But that was in the distant past, this afternoon, when I was tossed on the ocean of love's vagaries.

PAULINE: Eh?

ALAN: I was deranged, aberrant, demented.

PAULINE: I don't understand.

The doorbell sounds.

ALAN: Do you forgive me my love?

PAULINE: Well…

CHARLIE and DANGLE are willing an affirmative. DOLLY enters.

DOLLY: It's Lloyd, with a woman, and a man and Roscoe's minder.

CHARLIE: Shhh!!!

PAULINE: Let them in dad, please, I wanna know if Rachel's alright.

ALAN: "If Rachel's alright". What about me?!

CHARLIE/DANGLE: No! / Ohhhh!!

PAULINE: I do forgive you Alan. That's what love is innit. Forgiving someone when they've been a total dickhead.

ALAN: My heart is now in your hands. *(They kiss.)*

CHARLIE/DANGLE: Yes! / Done!

CHARLIE and DANGLE shake hands. Enter LLOYD, RACHEL, STANLEY and FRANCIS. Throughout the scene FRANCIS winks, nods at DOLLY.

LLOYD: Charlie.

CHARLIE: I want a word with you Lloydie? You're supposed to be my best mate –

LLOYD: – I –

CHARLIE: – Did you know about this!

LLOYD: Yessir, I did! What I did, I did for her. She's a great girl. She's like a daughter to me man!

RACHEL: I apologise, to you Alan, and to Charlie, for disguising myself as Roscoe.

CHARLIE: I guess it was the obvious thing to do, given you was identical twins.

DANGLE: Charlie, it is not possible to have *identical* twins of *different* sexes.

CHARLIE: *(Beat.)* You say that but –

DANGLE: – *Identical* comes from the Latin root "idem" meaning "the same" which has been bastardised in the English to "ident".

CHARLIE: What about "ical"? What does that mean?

LLOYD: Small! In Jamaican an ical bit of cake is a small piece of cake.

CHARLIE: Yeah, so *ident-ical* means "the same but an ical bit different". With identical twins that might mean the same but with some small differences.

DANGLE: *(Exasperated.)* Like sex?

CHARLIE: Yes.

RACHEL: I'll do this once Charlie and once only. Identical twins, also known as monozygotic twins, develop when a single sperm fertilises a single egg to form a single zygote, hence *mono zygote*, which then splits and forms two embryos which carry *identical* genetic material. Dizygotic twins, are formed when two separate eggs are fertilised by two separate sperm forming two separate zygotes. Twins of different sexes must be dizygotic, they cannot be monozygotic, identical twins, because they would have to be, by definition, of the same sex.

CHARLIE: *(Beat.)* What's your point?

ALL: Charlie?! / No! / Can we – Please! Listen! / Let me explain!

LLOYD: – Forget it! You're flogging a dead horse.

RACHEL: Charlie. This is Stanley.

PAULINE: *(To RACHEL.)* I'm so glad everything's worked out for you. I'm sorted with Alan now an'all.

CHARLIE: Yeah, it's all good. I'm glad it's sorted. I can relax now.

RACHEL: You still owe my family, me, six grand.

LLOYD: Fair do's. You can't argue with that Charlie.

CHARLIE: The money's not a problem Rachel, just give me a couple of years. *(Laughter.)* What?!

RACHEL: Stanley and I are going to get married.

CHARLIE: Congratulations.

RACHEL: And we're going to the police, to face the music.

LLOYD: You do right! The police love you. You rid the East End of Roscoe Crabbe!

STANLEY: I shall plead self-defence.

CHARLIE: What you need is a good attorney. This is Harry Dangle. He's the best. He got the Mau Mau off.

STANLEY: But in Kenya the Mau Mau killed a hundred thousand innocent men women and children.

DANGLE: Allegedly.

Gives his card to STANLEY.

I understand the only witness to the killing of Roscoe Crabbe was Rachel?

DANGLE: Who is also your intended?

STANLEY: Certainly.

DANGLE: In England a wife cannot give sworn evidence against her husband in a criminal trial.

STANLEY: What does that mean?

DANGLE: There are no witnesses to the crime.

STANLEY: But I did actually kill him.

CHARLIE: No! You plead not guilty.

STANLEY: But that would be lying.

CHARLIE: Lying ain't difficult. Here, give a go. Did you kill Roscoe Crabbe?

STANLEY: *(Beat.)* No.

PAULINE: Who killed him then?

ALAN: *(Defending her honour from the mob of the audience.)* Stupid, you cry?! I call it immaculate. Empty. Like a thermos.

DANGLE: The prospect of two weddings, and a court case with fees. What a wonderful day!

PAULINE takes DOLLY to one side.

PAULINE: *(To All, but mainly CHARLIE.)* Dad. It's all very well us all having an happy ending dad, but you ain't done nothing for Dolly.

CHARLIE: What's Dolly got to do with anything?

PAULINE: Rachel's minder has asked her to go on holiday. If you give her the time off, that's like three happy endings innit.

STANLEY: Wait! No! Dolly, listen. *(To DOLLY.)* Don't accept the first offer you get. You have a choice. Another man is in love with you and is offering a different kind of holiday.

DOLLY: You spend your whole life waiting for one man, then two come along at once.

ALAN: Like buses.

DOLLY: *(To STANLEY and RACHEL.)* What's the choice?

STANLEY: A traditional British dirty weekend in Margate. That's forty-eight hours with only a sex pest for company.

DOLLY: Sounds good, yeah. *(Beat.)* Or?

RACHEL: A romantic week abroad. Majorca.

DOLLY: That's a clear choice, now what about the men?

STANLEY: Paddy is offering Margate.

RACHEL: *(Indicating FRANCIS.)* Whereas with this man, next week, you'll be in Majorca in sunny Spain.

STANLEY: *(To FRANCIS.)* I thought you said the week after next?

FRANCIS: Let me try and explain.

RACHEL: I agreed that he could have next week off.

STANLEY: I've agreed that Henshall can have the week after next off, and I've paid him fifty pounds.

RACHEL: I've paid him fifty pounds and given him next week off.

DOLLY: Mm. Two weeks in Majorca.

TOGETHER: What's going on?

FRANCIS: It's all Paddy's fault –

STANLEY: – Where is Paddy?

FRANCIS: I think he's outside.

STANLEY: Go and get him.

(FRANCIS exits.)

CHARLIE: Dolly? Have you met this Paddy character.

DOLLY: Yeah. He's a bit of a charmer.

(Enter FRANCIS, no changes, except the accent.)

FRANCIS: *(Bad Irish accent.)* Now den dere? What's the craic?

RACHEL: Francis?

FRANCIS: No, I'm Paddy. If you want me bro he's outside.

CHARLIE: I know what's going on here. Are you and Francis monozygotic twins?

FRANCIS: That's it, yes we are!

STANLEY: Buzz wham! That explains everything!

Doorbell.

DOLLY: Except who that might be? I'll go.

Exit DOLLY.

CHARLIE: So this must be Paddy trying to come back in.

LLOYD: No man! This is Paddy.

FRANCIS: I'm Paddy.

DANGLE: Prove it?

FRANCIS: *(Singing.)* Oh Danny Boy, the pipes,

the pipes are calling,

From glen to glen, di da di da di da

Enter DOLLY followed by ALFIE. He carries a Thomas Cook's travel brochure.

DANGLE: He's definitely an Irishman.

LLOYD: Alfie! What are you doing here?

ALFIE: *(Not seeing FRANCIS.)* That lad Francis Henshall sent me with a message for someone called Dolly.

DOLLY: I'm Dolly.

ALFIE: Don't apologise. Paddy has died, so you can go on holiday with Francis to Majorca. Here. Page 62.

DOLLY: Oh.

STANLEY: *(Accusingly at FRANCIS.)* He died died, did he?

ALFIE: He did.

FRANCIS: Oh no.

RACHEL: *(At FRANCIS.)* What did he die of?

(All eyes on FRANCIS.)

FRANCIS: Vitamin D deficiency. Diagnosed as dermatitis.

DANGLE: Dermatitis is a dermatological disease.

LLOYD: You don't die of dermatitis!

FRANCIS: Dey do in Donegal. Dozens die daily.

STANLEY: But you're Paddy and you're not dead.

FRANCIS: Ah shit.

LLOYD: Man! What is it you don't understand?! Paddy never existed! Francis made Paddy up so's he could rip you both off for two salaries.

STANLEY: You two-timing little communist.

STANLEY swings a punch at FRANCIS who ducks and the punch contacts with ALFIE, knocking him clean out. He bounces back.

LLOYD: Are you alright Alfie?

ALFIE: Yeah, I'm getting used to it.

FRANCIS: Alright! I made Paddy up. I've been working for you, and simultaneously and at the same time for you. I'm only one man but I had two guvnors. I'm sorry you feel deceived, both of you, but I worked hard didn't I, I held down two jobs, and –

RACHEL: – nearly caused a double suicide.

FRANCIS: Only the man who never does nothing, never makes no mistakes. Judge me as you wished to be judged. Both of you have deceived people today for love. You guvnor, and you guvnor, you can't criticise me for doing the same, for I too have fallen in love.

PAULINE: With Alan?

LLOYD: He's right. There's no harm done.

RACHEL: I forgive you. You can have next week off.

STANLEY: I'd be a cad to complain. Take the week after next off too.

FRANCIS: Dolly? What do you say?

DOLLY: Charlie, can I have a fortnight holiday please. On full pay.

CHARLIE: Oh bloody hell. This happy ending's turning out expensive. Go on then.

LLOYD: Give her a kiss man!

STANLEY: Yummy!

FRANCIS kisses DOLLY. Applause and ooohs.

FRANCIS: *(Addressing the audience directly.)*

A bunk up in Majorca.
See sometimes, being a liar works.
And with dolly here – you have to say,
There's gotta be some fireworks.
I clocked on early, clocked off light.
Didn't eat til two.
I talked the talk and walked the walk.
And then I fell for you….
It's been a day of minor catastrophes

DOLLY: It's been a day of sink or swim

FRANCIS: I've done a lot of grovelling on my knees

DOLLY: I'd better go and shave my legs
Because I'm off to Spain with him

DOLLY/FRANCIS: Yesterday seems like last week
Last week seems like last year
But tomorrow looks good from here, oh yeah
Tomorrow looks good from here

STANLEY: I've been incognito and lying low

RACHEL: I've been dressed up as a man

STANLEY: There were times I thought you would never show

RACHEL: I can't wait to rip your clothes off

STANLEY/RACHEL: Gonna sort you when I can

STANLEY: Australia was looming dark

RACHEL: Australia was near

ALL: But tomorrow looks good from here, oh yeah
    Tomorrow looks good from here

ALAN: It's been a bus ride to hell and back again
    I felt like Mozart with just one hand
    But now she's mine I'm back on track again

PAULINE: A lot of stuff's been going on that I didn't understand
    Yesterday was lovely, yeah, today was nowhere near

ALL: But tomorrow looks good from here, oh yeah
    Tomorrow looks good from here.

DOLLY: I knew from the start that I would end up lovin' ya

FRANCIS: I'm only one man but I got two guvnors

Key change.

Tomorrow looks good from here oh yeah, tomorrow looks good from here.
Tomorrow looks good from hear oh yeah, tomorrow looks good from here – *(Claps.)*
Tomorrow looks good from hear oh yeah, tomorrow looks good from here
Tomorrow looks good from hear oh yeah, tomorrow looks good from here – *(Claps stop.)*
Tomorrow looks good, looks good, looks good from here.

The End.